Conflict and Compassion

Conflict and Compassion

a selection of poems edited by

JOHN SKULL

HUTCHINSON EDUCATIONAL

HUTCHINSON EDUCATIONAL LTD
178-202 Great Portland Street, London, W1

London Melbourne Sydney
Auckland Johannesburg Cape Town
and agencies throughout the world

First published July 1969
Second Impression March 1971

This book has been set in Plantin, printed in Great Britain by litho
by Anchor Press, and
bound by Wm. Brendon, both of Tiptree, Essex

ISBN 0 09 096060 2 (cased)
0 09 096061 0 (paper)

Contents

To show the structure of *Conflict and Compassion,* the sections only are given here. The poems are listed on pages 119–21.

1 Some of our human problems
'*Say obstacles exist they must encounter*' 1

2 The bomb
'*The bomb burst like a flower*' 9

3 War
'*It's the old game that was first played by Cain*' 25

4 Innocent victims of war
'*Man's forgetfulness of Man*' 35

5 The influence of environment
'*I know it was the place's fault*' 43

6 Social misfits
'*Oh lost and lonely one*' 51

7 Mental sickness
'*A matter hard to understand*' 59

8 Colour discrimination
'*When she had to sit beside a Negro*' 67

9 Road accidents
'*Registered, licensed homicide*' 75

10 Graver casualties
'*No more to build on there*' 81

11 Old age
'*The blight man was born for*' 89

12 Materialism
'*Our vast collective madness*' 95

13 Town 'planning'
'*Forests of unbudding stone*' 103

14 Humanity
'*This above all is precious*' 109

Index of first lines 117

List of poems 119

Acknowledgements 121

· TO BRENDA

'Say obstacles exist they must encounter'

I

Telling lies to the young is wrong

Telling lies to the young is wrong.
Proving to them that lies are true is wrong.
Telling them that God's in his heaven
and all's well with the world is wrong.
The young know what you mean. The young are people.
Tell them the difficulties can't be counted,
and let them see not only what will be
but see with clarity these present times.
Say obstacles exist they must encounter,
sorrow happens, hardship happens.
The hell with it. Who never knew
the price of happiness will not be happy.
Forgive no error you recognise,
it will repeat itself, increase,
and afterwards our pupils
will not forgive in us what we forgave.

                                        Y. Yevtushenko

Babel

There was a tower that went before a fall.
    Can't we ever, my love, speak in the same language?
Its nerves grew worse and worse as it grew tall.
    Have we no aims in common?

As children we are bickering over beads—
    Can't we ever, my love, speak in the same language?
The more there are together, Togetherness recedes.
    Have we no aims in common?

Exiles all as we are in a foreign city,
    Can't we ever, my love, speak in the same language?
We cut each other's throats out of our great self-pity—
    Have we no aims in common?

Patriots, dreamers, die-hards, theoreticians, all,
Can't we ever, my love, speak in the same language,
Or shall we go, still quarrelling over words, to the wall?
Have we no aims in common?

Louis Macneice

Of mourners

Mourn not for the man, speeding to lay waste
The essence of a countryside's most chaste
And ageless contour; her cool-breasted hills,
Purled streams, bare choirs in wood, fair daffodils—

Mourn not, as maudlin singers did, the scars
Left by the slag, industrial wars,
Men tearing fields apart for railway towns
Wresting the silly sheep from sleepy downs:

And sing no more the sentimental song
Of spinning jenny holding lads too long,
Of children toiling underground, or laws
For hanging witches, burning corn for cause.

Sing only with gibing Chaucer's tongue
Of foible and grave fault; of words unsung,
More pungent victory than battles won:
Sing deeds neglected, desecrations done

Not on the lovely body of the world
But on man's building heart, his shaping soul.
Mourn, with me, the intolerant, hater of sun:
Child's mind maimed before he learns to run.

Dorothy Livesay

4

Conclusion from **Autumn Journal**

What is it we want really?
  For what end and how?
If it is something feasible, obtainable,
  Let us dream it now,
And pray for a possible land
  Not of sleep-walkers, not of angry puppets,
But where both heart and brain can understand
  The movements of our fellows;
Where life is a choice of instruments and none
  Is debarred his natural music,
Where the waters of life are free of the ice-blockade of hunger
  And thought is free as the sun,
Where the altars of sheer power and mere profit
  Have fallen to disuse,
Where nobody sees the use
  Of buying money and blood at the cost of blood and money,
Where the individual, no longer squandered
  In self-assertion, works with the rest, endowed
With the split vision of a juggler and the quick lock of a taxi,
  Where the people are more than a crowd.
So sleep in hope of this—but only for a little;
  Your hope must wake
While the choice is yours to make,
  The mortgage not foreclosed, the offer open.
Sleep serene, avoid the backward
  Glance; go forward, dreams, and do not halt
(Behind you in the desert stands a token
  Of doubt—a pillar of salt).[1]
Sleep, the past, and wake, the future,
  And walk out promptly through the open door;
But you, my coward doubts, may go on sleeping,
  You need not wake again—not any more.
The New Year comes with bombs, it is too late
  To dose the dead with honourable intentions:
If you have honour to spare, employ it on the living;
  The dead are dead as 1938.

[1] *Genesis* XIX 26.

Sleep to the noise of running water
　　To-morrow to be crossed, however deep;
This is no river of the dead or Lethe,
　　To-night we sleep
On the banks of Rubicon—the die is cast;
　　There will be time to audit
The accounts later, there will be sunlight later
　　And the equation will come out at last.

Louis Macneice

Red balloon

It sailed across the startled town,
over chapels, over chimney-pots,
wind-blown above a block of flats
before it floated down.

Oddly, it landed where I stood,
and finding's keeping, as you know.
I breathed on it, I polished it,
till it shone like living blood.

It was my shame, it was my joy,
it brought me notoriety.
From all of Wales the rude boys came,
it ceased to be a toy.

I heard the girls of Cardiff sigh
when my balloon, my red balloon,
soared higher like a happiness
towards the dark blue sky.

Nine months since, I have boasted of
my unique, my only precious;
but to no one dare I show it now
however long they swear their love.

'It's a Jew's balloon,' my best friend cried,
'stained with our dear Lord's blood.'
'That I'm a Jew is true,' I said,
said I, 'that cannot be denied.'

'What relevance?' I asked surprised,
'what's religion to do with this?'
'Your red balloon's a Jew's balloon,
let's get it circumcised.'

Then some boys laughed and some boys cursed,
some unsheathed their dirty knives:
some lunged, some clawed at my balloon,
but still it would not burst.

They bled my nose, they cut my eye,
half conscious in the street I heard,
'Give up, give up your red balloon,'
I don't know exactly why.

Father, bolt the door, turn the key,
lest those sad, brash boys return
to insult my faith and steal
my red balloon from me.

                                        Dannie Abse

Epitaph

I think they will remember this as the age of lamentations,
The age of broken minds and broken souls,
The age of hurt creatures sobbing out their sorrow to the
    rhythm of the blues—
The music of lost Africa's desolation become the music of the
    town.

The age of failure of splendid things,
The age of the deformity of splendid things,
The age of old young men and bitter children,
The age of treachery and of a great new faith.
The age of madness and machines,
Of broken bodies and fear twisted hearts,

The age of frenzied fumbling and possessive lusts—
And yet, deep down, an age unsatisfied by dirt and guns,
An age which though choked by the selfishness of the few who
    owned their bodies and their souls,
Still struggled blindly to the end,
And in their time reached out magnificently
Even for the very stars themselves.

                      H. D. Carberry

'*The bomb burst like a flower*'

2

Hiroshima

The bomb burst like a flower,
And grew upwards under the sun.
And men stood afar off, and wondered
What was the meaning of this?
Then the flower died, and they partly forgot
What had happened that summer day.
But in later years terror reigned in the land,
For the deadly blight of the flower had fallen on men,
And as they died, they cried to the stars to avenge
This inhumanity of man to man.

And future generations inherited
A sorrow, and a remembrance of it,
And a lesson drawn from their ancestors' futility.

Angela M. Clifton

Hiroshima

When in the aftermath
They come to stir the dust
And shards[1] of an old myth
Will they pause before the shape
Of a prone man bitten
By the acid of the lie
Into the coffin step?
What will it mean to them
That a culture had to die
To bequeath that lightning-written
Cryptograph[2] of stone,
That fossil shame?

O cry it across the chasm
Of ages, how we struck
In the atom's smithy a sword

[1] shards: fragments, broken bits.
[2] Cryptograph: secret writings; something written in such a way that a key is needed to interpret it.

That kissed with a comet's breath,
And the town conceived death
In a cyclopean[1] orgasm.[2]
Tell how we bent the knee
To the image of our power,
The blood-fed Upas tree[3]
With its crown against the sky
And root clenched in the bone
Of the wronged and the wrongdoer.

Speak, lips of stone,
And make the ravished town
The bride of Sinai.[4]

                                        Stanley Snaith

No more Hiroshimas

At the station exit, my bundle in hand,
Early the winter afternoon's wet snow
Falls thinly round me, out of a crudded[5] sun.
I had forgotten to remember where I was.
Looking about, I see it might be anywhere—
A station, a town like any other in Japan,
Ramshackle, muddy, noisy, drab; a cheerfully
Shallow permanence: peeling concrete, litter, 'Atomic
Lotion, for hair fall-out,' a flimsy department-store;
Racks and towers of neon, flashy over tiled and tilted waves
Of little roofs, shacks cascading lemons and persimmons,[6]
Oranges and dark-red apples, shanties awash with rainbows

---

[1] cyclopean: huge—like the one-eyed giant Cyclops of Greek mythology.
[2] orgasm: expression of violent excitement especially that at the height of intensity in the sexual act.
[3] Upas tree: a tree something like a fig tree, which yields a poisonous, milky sap. It was believed to destroy every living thing within miles.
[4] bride of Sinai: the idea is that what happened at Hiroshima and on Mount Sinai should be 'married' in people's minds. The stones of Hiroshima should speak redemptively to the world, as did the stone tablets brought down from Mount Sinai.
[5] crudded: looking like cheese or curd.
[6] persimmons: a plum-like fruit. The Japanese variety is red.

Of squid and octopus, shellfish, slabs of tuna, oysters, ice,
Ablaze with fans of soiled nude-picture books
Thumbed abstractedly by schoolboys, with second-hand looks.

The river remains unchanged, sad, refusing rehabilitation.
In this long, wide, empty official boulevard
The new trees are still small, the office blocks
Basely functional, the bridge a slick abstraction.
But the river remains unchanged, sad, refusing rehabilitation.

In the city centre, far from the station's lively squalor,
A kind of life goes on, in cinemas and hi-fi coffee bars,
In the shuffling racket of pin-table palaces and parlours,
The souvenir-shops piled with junk, kimonoed kewpie-dolls,
Models of the bombed Industry Promotion Hall, memorial ruin
Tricked out with glitter-frost and artificial pearls.

Set in an awful emptiness, the modern tourist hotel is trimmed
With jaded Christmas frippery, flatulent balloons; in the hall,
A giant dingy iced cake in the shape of a Cinderella coach.
The contemporary stairs are treacherous, the corridors
Deserted, my room an overheated morgue, the bar in darkness.
Punctually, the electric chimes ring out across the tidy waste
Their doleful public hymn—the tune unrecognisable, evangelist.

Here atomic peace is geared to meet the tourist trade.
Let it remain like this, for all the world to see,
Without nobility or loveliness, and dogged with shame
That is beyond all hope of indignation. Anger, too, is dead.
And why should memorials of what was far
From pleasant have the grace that helps us to forget?

In the dying afternoon, I wander dying round the Park of Peace.
It is right, this squat, dead place, with its left-over air
Of an abandoned International Trade and Tourist Fair.
The stunted trees are wrapped in straw against the cold.
The gardeners are old, old women in blue bloomers, white aprons,
Survivors weeding the dead brown lawns around the Children's
    Monument.

A hideous pile, the Atomic Bomb Explosion Centre, freezing cold,
'Includes the Peace Tower, a museum containing
Atomic-melted slates and bricks, photos showing
What the Atomic Desert looked like, and other
Relics of the catastrophe.'

The other relics:
The ones that made me weep;
The bits of burnt clothing,
The stopped watches, the torn shirts.
The twisted buttons,
The stained and tattered vests and drawers,
The ripped kimonos and charred boots,
The white blouse polka-dotted with atomic rain, indelible,
The cotton summer pants the blasted boys crawled home in, to
    bleed
And slowly die.

Remember only these.
They are the memorials we need.

James Kirkup

Parable

Two neighbours, who were rather dense,
Considered that their mutual fence
Were more symbolic of their peace
(Which they maintained should never cease)
If each about his house and garden
Set up a more substantial warden.
Quickly they cleared away the fence
To build a wall at great expense;
And soon their little plots of ground
Were barricaded all around:
Yet still they added stone to stone,
As if they never would be done,
For when one neighbour seemed to tire
The other shouted: Higher! Higher!

Thus day by day, in their unease,
They built the battlements of peace
Whose shadows, like a gathering blot,
Darkened on each neglected plot,
Until the ground, so overcast,
Became a rank and weedy waste.

Now in obsession, they uprear;
Jealous, and proud, and full of fear:
And, lest they halt for lack of stone,
They pull their dwelling-houses down.
At last, by their insane excess,
Their ramparts guard a wilderness;
And hate, arousing out of shame,
Flares up into a wondrous flame:
They curse; they strike; they break the wall
Which buries them beneath its fall.

William Soutar

The unexploded bomb

Two householders (semi-detached) once found,
Digging their gardens, a bomb underground—
Half in one's land, half in t'other's, with the fence between.
Neighbours they were, but for years had been
Hardly on speaking terms. Now X. unbends
To pass a remark across the creosoted fence:
'Look what I've got! . . . Oh, you've got it too.
Then what, may I ask, are you proposing to do
About this object of yours which menaces my wife,
My kiddies, my property, my whole way of life?'
'Your way of life,' says Y., 'is no credit to humanity.
I don't wish to quarrel; but, since you began it, I
Find your wife stuck-up, your children repel me,
And let me remind you that we too have the telly.
This bomb of mine—'
                          'I don't like your tone!
And I must point out that, since I own

More bomb than you, to create any tension
Between us won't pay you.'
                              'What a strange misapprehension!'
Says the other: 'my portion of bomb is near
Six inches longer than yours. So there!'

'They seem,' the bomb muttered in its clenched and narrow
Sleep, 'to take me for a vegetable marrow.'

'It would give me,' said X., 'the very greatest pleasure
To come across the fence now with my tape-measure—'
'Oh no,' Y. answered, 'I'm not having you
Trampling my flowerbeds and peering through
My windows.'
                    'Oho,' snarled X., 'if that's
Your attitude, I warn you to keep your brats
In future from trespassing upon my land,
Or they'll bitterly regret it.'
                              'You misunderstand.
My family has no desire to step on
Your soil; and my bomb is a peace-lover's weapon.'

Called a passing angel, 'If you two shout
And fly into tantrums and keep dancing about,
The thing will go off. It is surely permissible
To say that your bomb, though highly fissible,
Is in another sense one and indivisible;
By which I mean—if you'll forgive the phrase,
Gentlemen—the bloody thing works both ways.
So let me put forward a dispassionate proposal:
Both of you, ring for a bomb-disposal
Unit, and ask them to remove post-haste
The cause of your dispute.'

                    X. and Y. stared aghast
At the angel. 'Remove my bomb?' they sang
In unison both: 'allow a gang
To invade my garden and pull up the fence
Upon which my whole way of life depends?

Only a sentimental idealist
Could moot it. I, thank God, am a realist.'

The angel fled. The bomb turned over
In its sleep and mumbled, 'I shall soon discover,
If X. and Y. are too daft to unfuse me,
How the Devil intends to use me.'

C. Day Lewis

This excellent machine

This excellent machine is neatly planned,
A child, a half-wit would not feel perplexed:
No chance to err, you simply press the button—
At once each cog in motion moves the next,
The whole revolves, and anything that lives
Is quickly sucked towards the running band,
Where, shot between the automatic knives,
It's guaranteed to finish dead as mutton.

This excellent machine will illustrate
The modern world divided into nations:
So neatly planned, that if you merely tap it
The armaments will start their devastations,
And though we're for it, though we're all convinced
Some fool will press the button soon or late,
We stand and stare, expecting to be minced,—
And very few are asking *Why not scrap it?*

John Lehmann

Peach, Plum, or Apricot

Peach, Plum, or Apricot!
How much money have you got?
If you've got a bob or two,
I will bring some home for you.

Apricot, Peach, or Plum!
We may get blown to kingdom come,
Let us eat our fruit before
Our parents go again to war.

Plum, Apricot, or Peach!
Hide the stone from out their reach,
So that it falls into the earth
And brings another world to birth.

Bernard Kops

Fifteen million plastic bags

I was walking in a government warehouse
Where the daylight never goes.
I saw fifteen million plastic bags
Hanging in a thousand rows.

Five million bags were six feet long
Five million bags were five foot five
Five million were stamped with Mickey Mouse
And they came in a smaller size.

Were they for guns or uniforms
Or a kinky kind of party game?
Then I saw each bag had a number
And every bag bore a name.

And five million bags were six feet long
Five million were five foot five
Five million were stamped with Mickey Mouse
And they came in a smaller size.

So I've taken my bag from the hanger
And I've pulled it over my head
And I'll wait for the priest to zip it
So the radiation won't spread.

Now five million bags are six feet long
Five million are five foot five
Five million are stamped with Mickey Mouse
And they come in a smaller size.

Adrian Mitchell

Your attention please

The Polar DEW has just warned that
A nuclear rocket strike of
At least one thousand megatons
Has been launched by the enemy
Directly at our major cities.
This announcement will take
Two and a quarter minutes to make,
You therefore have a further
Eight and a quarter minutes
To comply with the shelter
Requirements published in the Civil
Defence Code—section Atomic Attack.
A specially shortened Mass
Will be broadcast at the end
Of this announcement—
Protestant and Jewish services
Will begin simultaneously—
Select your wavelength immediately
According to instructions
In the Defence Code. Do not
Take well-loved pets (including birds)
Into your shelter—they will consume
Fresh air. Leave the old and bed-
ridden, you can do nothing for them.
Remember to press the sealing
Switch when everyone is in
The shelter. Set the radiation
Aerial, turn on the geiger barometer.

Turn off your Television now.
Turn off your radio immediately
The Services end. At the same time
Secure explosion plugs in the ears
Of each member of your family. Take
Down your plasma flasks. Give your children
The pills marked one and two
In the C.D. green container, then put
Them to bed. Do not break
The inside airlock seals until
The radiation All Clear shows
(Watch for the cuckoo in your
perspex panel), or your District
Touring Doctor rings your bell.
If before this, your air becomes
Exhausted or if any of your family
Is critically injured, administer
The capsules marked 'Valley Forge'
(Red pocket in No. 1 Survival Kit)
For painless death. (Catholics
Will have been instructed by their priests
What to do in this eventuality.)
This announcement is ending. Our President
Has already given orders for
Massive retaliation—it will be
Decisive. Some of us may die.
Remember, statistically
It is not likely to be you.
All flags are flying fully dressed
On Government buildings—the sun is shining.
Death is the least we have to fear.
We are all in the hands of God,
Whatever happens happens by His Will.
Now go quickly to your shelters.

Peter Porter

The horses

Barely a twelvemonth after
The seven days war that put the world to sleep,
Late in the evening the strange horses came.
By then we had made our covenant with silence,
But in the first few days it was so still
We listened to our breathing and were afraid.
On the second day
The radios failed; we turned the knobs; no answer.
On the third day a warship passed us, heading north,
Dead bodies piled on the deck. On the sixth day
A plane plunged over us into the sea. Thereafter
Nothing. The radios dumb;
And still they stand in corners of our kitchens,
And stand, perhaps, turned on, in a million rooms
All over the world. But now if they should speak,
If on a sudden they should speak again,
If on the stroke of noon a voice should speak,
We would not listen, we would not let it bring
That old bad world that swallowed its children quick
At one great gulp. We would not have it again.
Sometimes we think of the nations lying asleep,
Curled blindly in impenetrable sorrow,
And then the thought confounds us with its strangeness.

The tractors lie about our fields; at evening
They look like dank sea-monsters couched and waiting.
We leave them where they are and let them rust:
'They'll moulder away and be like other loam.'
We make our oxen drag our rusty ploughs,
Long laid aside. We have gone back
Far past our fathers' land.
                              And then, that evening
Late in the summer the strange horses came.
We heard a distant tapping on the road,
A deepening drumming; it stopped, went on again
And at the corner changed to hollow thunder.
We saw the heads

Like a wild wave charging and were afraid.
We had sold our horses in our fathers' time
To buy new tractors. Now they were strange to us
As fabulous steeds set on an ancient shield
Or illustrations in a book of knights.
We did not dare go near them. Yet they waited,
Stubborn and shy, as if they had been sent
By an old command to find our whereabouts
And that long-lost archaic companionship.
In the first moment we had never a thought
That they were creatures to be owned and used.
Among them were some half-a-dozen colts
Dropped in some wilderness of the broken world,
Yet new as if they had come from their own Eden.
Since then they have pulled our ploughs and borne our loads,
But that free servitude still can pierce our hearts.
Our life is changed; their coming our beginning.

Edwin Muir

The responsibility

I am the man who gives the word,
If it should come, to use the Bomb.
I am the man who spreads the word
From him to them if it should come.

I am the man who gets the word
From him who spreads the word from him.

I am the man who drops the Bomb
If ordered by the one who's heard
From him who merely spreads the word
The first one gives if it should come.

I am the man who loads the Bomb
That he must drop should orders come
From him who gets the word passed on
By one who waits to hear from *him*.

I am the man who makes the Bomb
That he must load for him to drop
If told by one who gets the word
From one who passes it from *him*.

I am the man who fills the till,
Who pays the tax, who foots the bill
That guarantees the Bomb he makes
For him to load for him to drop
If orders come from one who gets
The word passed on to him by one
Who waits to hear it from the man
Who gives the word to use the Bomb.

I am the man behind it all;
I am the one responsible.

Peter Appleton

'*It's the old game that was first played by Cain*'

3

The airman

I do not know—would that I knew!—
To what end I have learnt this skill,
Or why I climb each day into the sky
To find one who shall kill me, or to kill.
If only we might think it true
That it's a simple thing to die
In a good cause—both he and I!
But that's not so. Too well we know
It's the old game that was first played by Cain,
By Greek and Trojan, English, French and Scot,
Again and yet again,
And all—for any good the world has got—
Except for the game's sake, always in vain.
Then to no end, for no cause, without hate
We two shall meet among the clouds, and fall,
Since to our death, one or both, fall we must.
And yet, can that be all?
Out of the dust of him who dies
This time let no avenger rise;
But somehow, some day, soon or late
Since all things change and wax and wane,
And happiness is the child of pain,
May it not be that those born after,
Because we lived and fought and died
Led by hope, not by hate or pride,
Shall grow wise and return to laughter?

R. C. Trevelyan

The scene of war: the happy warrior

His wild heart beats with painful sobs
his stain'd hands clench an ice-cold rifle
his aching jaws grip a hot parch'd tongue
his wide eyes search unconsciously.

He cannot shriek

Bloody saliva
dribbles down his shapeless jacket.

I saw him stab
and stab again
a well-killed Boche.

This is the happy warrior,
this is he. . . .   *Herbert Read*

Bayonet charge

Suddenly he awoke and was running—raw
In raw-seamed hot khaki, his sweat heavy,
Stumbling across a field of clods towards a green hedge
That dazzled with rifle fire, hearing
Bullets smacking the belly out of the air—
He lugged a rifle numb as a smashed arm;
The patriotic tear that had brimmed in his eye
Sweating like molten iron from the centre of his chest—

In bewilderment then he almost stopped—
In what cold clockwork of the stars and the nations
Was he the hand pointing that second? He was running
Like a man who has jumped up in the dark and runs
Listening between his footfalls for the reason
Of his still running, and his foot hung like
Statuary in mid-stride. Then the shot-slashed furrows

Threw up a yellow hare that rolled like a flame
And crawled in a threshing circle, its mouth wide
Open silent, its eyes standing out.
He plunged past with his bayonet towards the green hedge.
King, honour, human dignity, etcetera
Dropped like luxuries in a yelling alarm
To get out of that blue crackling air
His terror's touchy dynamite.   *Ted Hughes*

28

The sentry

We'd found an old Boche dug-out, and he knew,
And gave us hell, for shell on frantic shell
Hammered on top, but never quite burst through.
Rain, guttering down in waterfalls of slime,
Kept slush waist-high and rising hour by hour,
And choked the steps too thick with clay to climb.
What murk of air remained stank old, and sour
With fumes of whizz-bangs, and the smell of men
Who'd lived there years, and left their curse in the den,
If not their corpses. . . .

              There we herded from the blast
Of whizz-bangs, but one found our door at last,—
Buffeting eyes and breath, snuffing the candles,
And thud! flump! thud! down the steep steps came thumping
And sploshing in the flood, deluging muck—
The sentry's body; then, his rifle, handles
Of old Boche bombs, and mud in ruck on ruck.
We dredged him up, for killed, until he whined
'O sir, my eyes—I'm blind—I'm blind, I'm blind!'
Coaxing, I held a flame against his lids
And said if he could see the least blurred light
He was not blind; in time he'd get all right.
'I can't,' he sobbed. Eyeballs, huge-bulged like squids',
Watch my dreams still; but I forgot him there
In posting Next for duty, and sending a scout
To beg a stretcher somewhere, and flound'ring about
To other posts under the shrieking air.

          *   *   *

Those other wretches, how they bled and spewed,
And one who would have drowned himself for good,—
I try not to remember these things now.
Let dread hark back for one word only: how
Half listening to that sentry's moans and jumps,
And the wild chattering of his broken teeth,

Renewed most horribly whenever crumps
Pummelled the roof and slogged the air beneath—
Through the dense din, I say, we heard him shout
'I see your lights!' But ours had long died out.

Wilfred Owen

Does it matter?

Does it matter?—losing your leg? . . .
For people will always be kind,
And you need not show that you mind
When the others come in after hunting
To gobble their muffins and eggs.

Does it matter?—losing your sight? . . .
There's such splendid work for the blind;
And people will always be kind,
As you sit on the terrace remembering
And turning your face to the light.

Do they matter?—those dreams from the pit? . . .
You can drink and forget and be glad,
And people won't say that you're mad;
For they'll know that you've fought for your country,
And no one will worry a bit.

Siegfried Sassoon

Where have all the flowers gone?

Where have all the flowers gone?
Long time passing.
Where have all the flowers gone?
Long time ago.
Where have all the flowers gone?
Young girls picked them, every one.
When will they ever learn,
O when will they ever learn.

Where have all the young girls gone?
Long time passing.
Where have all the young girls gone?
Long time ago.
Where have all the young girls gone?
Gone to young men, every one.
When will they ever learn,
O when will they ever learn.

Where have all the young men gone?
Long time passing.
Where have all the young men gone?
Long time ago.
Where have all the young men gone?
Gone for soldiers, every one.
When will they ever learn,
O when will they ever learn.

Where have all the soldiers gone?
Long time passing.
Where have all the soldiers gone?
Long time ago.
Where have all the soldiers gone?
Gone to graveyards, every one.
When will they ever learn,
O when will they ever learn.

Where have all the graveyards gone?
Long time passing.
Where have all the graveyards gone?
Long time ago.
Where have all the graveyards gone?
Gone to flower, every one.
When will they ever learn,
O when will they ever learn.

Where have all the flowers gone?
Long time passing.
Where have all the flowers gone?
Long time ago.
Where have all the flowers gone?
Young girls picked them, every one.
When will they ever learn,
O when will they ever learn.

Pete Seeger

After a war

The outcome? Conflicting rumours
As to what faction murdered
The one man who, had he survived,
Might have ruled us without corruption.
Not that it matters now:
We're busy collecting the dead,
Counting them, hard though it is
To be sure what side they were on.
What's left of their bodies and faces
Tells of no need but for burial,
And mutilation was practised
By Right, Left and Centre alike.
As for the children and women
Who knows what they wanted
Apart from the usual things?
Food is scarce now, and men are scarce,
Whole villages burnt to the ground,
New cities in disrepair.

The war is over. Somebody must have won.
Somebody will have won, when peace is declared.

Michael Hamburger

Will it be so again?

Will it be so again
That the brave, the gifted are lost from view,
And empty, scheming men
Are left in peace their lunatic age to renew?
Will it be so again?

Must it be always so
That the best are chosen to fall and sleep
Like seeds, and we too slow
In claiming the earth they quicken, and the old usurpers reap
What they could not sow?

Will it be so again—
The jungle code and the hypocrite gesture?
A poppy wreath for the slain
And a cut-throat world for the living? That stale imposture
Played on us once again?

Will it be as before—
Peace, with no heart or mind to ensue it,
Guttering down to war
Like a libertine to his grave? We should not be surprised: we
    knew it
Happen before.

Shall it be so again?
Call not upon the glorious dead
To be your witnesses then.
The living alone can nail to their promise the ones who said
It shall not be so again.

C. Day Lewis

'Man's forgetfulness of man'

4

Associated Press Ltd: Wounded family in South Vietnam

The war orphans

Written after seeing a photograph of Korean children asleep in the snow.

The snow is the blood of these poor Dead . . . they have no
    other—
These children, old in the dog's scale of years, too old
For the hopeless breast—ghosts for whom there is none to care,
Grown fleshless as the skeleton
Of Adam, they have known
More aeons[1] of cold than he endured
In the first grave of the world. They have, for bed,
The paving stones, the spider spins their blankets, and their
    bread
Is the shred and crumb of dead Chance. In this epoch of the cold,
In which new worlds are formed, new glaciations
To overcast the world that was the heart,
There is only that architecture of the winter, the huge plan
Of the lasting skeleton, built from the hunger of Man,
Constructed for hunger—piteous in its griefs, the humiliation
Of outworn flesh, the Ape-cerement,[2] O the foolish tattered
    clothing,
Rags stained with the filth of humanity, stink of its toiling,
But never the smell of the heart, with its warmth, its fevers,
Rapacity and grandeur. For the cold is zero
In infinite intensity, brother to democratic
Death, our one equality, who holds
Alike the maelstrom[3] of the blood, the world's incendiarism,
The summer redness and the hope of the rose,
The beast, and man's superiority o'er the beast
That is but this:
Man bites with his smile, and poisons with his kiss.

[1] aeons: an age, a vast, almost immeasurable period of time.

[2] Ape-cerement: cerements were waxed burial clothes. Here the pallid skins of the orphans are like the shrouds that covered the dead.

[3] maelstrom: a terrifying whirlpool; a powerful influence for destruction. Here it means the violence that exists in human emotions.

When, in each dawn,
The light on my brow is changed to the mark of Cain,
And my blood cries 'Am I my brother's keeper?' seeing these
    ghosts
Of Man's forgetfulness of Man, I feel again
The pitiless but healing rain—who thought I only
Had the lonely Lethe[1] flood for tears.

Edith Sitwell

Algerian refugee camp, Aïn Khemouda

You have black eyes,
Four years of age,
A chic, cast-off coat
—pepper-and-salt, double-breasted—
A label naming you 'Mohammed',
Some slippers, a squashed felt hat.
Nothing else. And 'nothing' means just that.

This camp is your home until—well, until.
A flag flaps on a hill.
The *oued*[2] soon will be dry;
Do you know how to cry?

Smoke curls from the tents
Where women who are not your mother,
Hennaed[3] and trinketed, cook.
Your eyes see but do not look.
And men who are not your father,
Turbaned and burned, sit stiff
In rows, like clay pigeons, on a cliff.
Targets do not easily relax.
Your hair is fair as flax.

[1] Lethe: the river of forgetfulness in ancient Greek mythology.
[2] *oued*: a wadi or river bed which is dry, except in the rainy season.
[3] Hennaed: dyed with henna. Many Eastern women stain their nails,
eyelids and hair with the reddish dye obtained from the leaves of henna.

Guns rattle the mauve hills
Where the last warmth spills
On villages where once you were
One of a family that died.
Not much else. Just that.

You pull down the brim of your hat.
I do not know what goes on inside?

Alan Ross

Bombing casualties in Spain

Dolls' faces are rosier but these were children
their eyes not glass but gleaming gristle
dark lenses in whose quicksilvery glances
the sunlight quivered. These blench'd lips
were warm once and bright with blood
but blood
held in a moist bleb of flesh
not spilt and spatter'd in tousled hair.

In these shadowy tresses
red petals did not always
thus clot and blacken to a scar.
These are dead faces.
Wasps' nests are not more wanly waxen
wood embers not so greyly ashen.

They are laid out in ranks
like paper lanterns that have fallen
after a night of riot
extinct in the dry morning air.

Herbert Read

Refugee blues

Say this city has ten million souls,
Some are living in mansions, some are living in holes:
Yet there's no place for us, my dear, yet there's no place for us.

39

Once we had a country and we thought it fair,
Look in the atlas and you'll find it there:
We cannot go there now, my dear, we cannot go there now.

In the village churchyard there grows an old yew,
Every spring it blossoms anew:
Old passports can't do that, my dear, old passports can't do that.

The consul banged the table and said;
'If you've got no passport, you're officially dead':
But we are still alive, my dear, but we are still alive.

Went to a committee; they offered me a chair;
Asked me politely to return next year:
But where shall we go to-day, my dear, but where shall we go
    to-day?

Came to a public meeting; the speaker got up and said:
'If we let them in, they will steal our daily bread';
He was talking of you and me, my dear, he was talking of you and
    me.

Thought I heard the thunder rumbling in the sky;
It was Hitler over Europe, saying: 'They must die';
O we were in his mind, my dear, O we were in his mind.

Saw a poodle in a jacket fastened with a pin,
Saw a door opened and a cat let in:
But they weren't German Jews, my dear, but they weren't
    German Jews.

Went down the harbour and stood upon the quay,
Saw the fish swimming as if they were free:
Only ten feet away, my dear, only ten feet away.

Walked through a wood, saw the birds in the trees;
They had no politicians and sang at their ease:
They weren't the human race, my dear, they weren't the human
    race.

Dreamed I saw a building with a thousand floors,
A thousand windows and a thousand doors;
Not one of them was ours, my dear, not one of them was ours.

Stood on a great plain in the falling snow;
Ten thousand soldiers marched to and fro:
Looking for you and me, my dear, looking for you and me.

W. H. Auden

Homesick

I've lived in the ghetto[1] here more than a year,
In Terezın, in the black town now,
And when I remember my old home so dear,
I can love it more than I did, somehow.

Ah, home, home,
Why did they tear me away?
Here the weak die easy as a feather
And when they die, they die forever.

I'd like to go back home again,
It makes me think of sweet spring flowers.
Before, when I used to live at home,
It never seemed so dear and fair.

I remember now those golden days . . .
But maybe I'll be going there soon again.

---

[1] ghetto: a part of a town or city in which Jews were formerly confined.
Here it refers to the concentration camp.

People walk along the street,
You see at once on each you meet
That there's a ghetto here,
A place of evil and of fear.
There's little to eat and much to want,
Where bit by bit, it's horror to live.
But no one must give up!
The world turns and times change.

Yet we all hope the time will come
When we'll go home again.
Now I know how dear it is
And often I remember it.

Anonymous

(Written by a child in Theresienstadt Concentration Camp, 1943.)

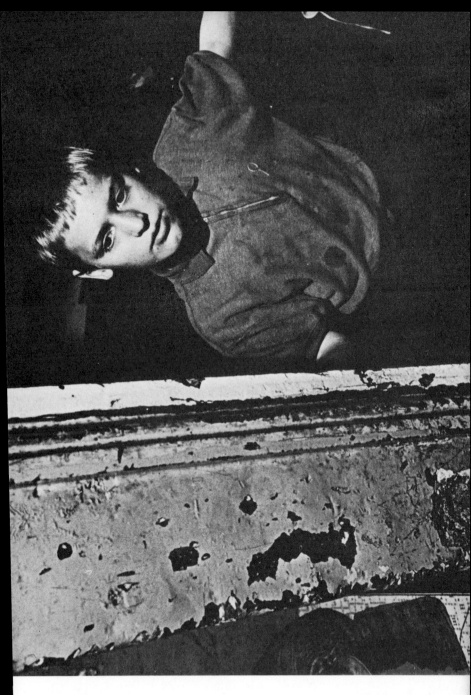

'I know it was the place's fault'

5

Photograph by Nick Hedges: London

The place's fault

Once, after a rotten day at school—
Sweat on my fingers, pages thumbed with smears,
Cane smashing down to make me keep them neat—
I blinked out to the sunlight and the heat
And stumbled up the hill, still swallowing tears.
A stone hissed past my ear—'Yah! gurt fat fool!'

Some urchins waited for me by my gate.
I shouted swear-words at them, walked away.
'Yeller,' they yelled, ' 'e's yeller!' And they flung
Clods, stones, bricks—anything to make me run.
I ran, all right, up hill all scorching day
With 'yeller' in my ears. 'I'm not, I'm not!'

Another time, playing too near the shops—
Oddly, no doubt, I'm told I was quite odd,
Making, no doubt, a noise—a girl in slacks
Came out and told some kids 'Run round the back,
Bash in his back door, smash up his back yard,
And if he yells I'll go and fetch the cops.'

And what a rush I had to lock those doors
Before that rabble reached them! What desire
I've had these twenty years to lock away
That place where fingers pointed out my play,
Where even the grass was tangled with barbed wire,
Where through the streets I waged continual wars!

We left (it was a temporary halt)
The knots of ragged kids, the wired-off beach,
Faces behind the blinds. I'll not return;
There's nothing there I haven't had to learn,
And I've learned nothing that I'd care to teach—
Except that I know it was the place's fault.

Philip Hobsbaum

My parents kept me from children who were rough

My parents kept me from children who were rough
And who threw words like stones and who wore torn clothes.
Their thighs showed through rags. They ran in the street
And climbed cliffs and stripped by the country streams.

I feared more than tigers their muscles like iron
And their jerking hands and their knees tight on my arms.
I feared the salt coarse pointing of those boys
Who copied my lisp behind me on the road.

They were lithe, they sprang out behind hedges
Like dogs to bark at our world. They threw mud
And I looked another way, pretending to smile.
I longed to forgive them, yet they never smiled.

Stephen Spender

Incendiary

That one small boy with a face like pallid cheese
And burnt-out little eyes could make a blaze
As brazen, fierce and huge, as red and gold
And zany[1] yellow as the one that spoiled
Three thousand guineas' worth of property
And crops at Goodwin's Farm on Saturday
Is frightening, as fact and metaphor:
An ordinary match intended for
The lighting of a pipe or kitchen fire
Misused may set a whole menagerie
Of flame-fanged tigers roaring hungrily.
And frightening, too, that one small boy should set
The sky on fire and choke the stars to heat
Such skinny limbs and such a little heart
Which would have been content with one warm kiss,
Had there been anyone to offer this.

Vernon Scannell

[1] Zany: crazy.

46

On the death of a murderer

'One day Vera showed us a photograph of some local Gestapo men
which had come into her hands. The photograph had been taken when
they were in the country outside Prague for a day's holiday. The
young men were ranged in two rows in their neat uniforms, and they
stared out at us with professionally menacing but unhappy eyes
from that recent past now dead.
'... After the relief of Prague these young men were hunted through
the countryside, Vera told us, like wild game, and all of them taken
and killed.'

EDWIN MUIR, *Autobiography*

Over the hill the city lights leap up.
But there in the fields the quiet dusk folds down.
A man lies in a ditch. He listens hard.
His own fast breathing is the biggest sound,
But through it, coming nearer, he hears another:
The voices of his hunters, coming nearer.

They are coming, and he can run no further.

He was born in a Germany thrashing like a fish
On a gravel towpath beating out its life.
As a child, something they called the Blockade[1]
Nearly strangled him with impersonal cold fingers.
Clever doctors saved his life. The Blockade receded.
He hopped in the Berlin streets like a cool sparrow.
His wise friends showed him a quick way to earn
Pocket-money: while English schoolboys chalked
Dirty words and sniggered behind desk-lids,
He learnt the things the words meant; his pockets
Filled up with change and his heart jingled with hate.

Now his hate has jingled in the ears of Europe.
He has taught them to know the refusal of pity.
His life is nearly over; only the darkness

[1] Blockade: during the Second World War the British Navy attempted
to prevent ('blockade') ships bringing supplies to Germany. The Blockade resulted in a shortage of food and other necessities in Germany.

47

Covers him as his pursuers cry over the fields.
In a moment they will tear him to pieces.
He was sick of the things that went with the dirty words:
Sick of the pocket-money and the windy street.
Then the uniforms came. They said to him: *Be strong*.

When he was fifteen, he had a gun.
He had forgotten the Blockade and the pocket-money,
Except on nights when he could not sleep: his gun
Was a friend, but when they gave him a whip
He loved that better still. *Be strong !* He cried.

The speeches were made, the leaves fell, it was war.
To smashed Prague his gun and his whip led him in time.
There, he learnt the delight of refusing pity.

Did he never wonder about those he murdered?
Never feel curious about the severe light
That flamed in their irises as they lay dying?
Apparently not. His duty took all his care.
He fed his starving heart with cruelty
Till it got sick and died. His masters applauded.
Once, he dragged off a man's lower jaw.

Now they are coming nearer over the fields.
It is like the Blockade, only worse. He will die.
They have taken away his whip and gun.

But let us watch the scene with a true eye,
Arrest your pen, hurrying chronicler.
Do you take this for a simple act: the mere
Crushing of a pest that crawled on the world's hide?
Look again: is there not an ironic light
In the fiery sky that rings his desperate head?

He will die, this cursed man. The first pursuer
Is here. The darkness is ready to give him up.
He has, at most, a hundred breaths to draw.
But what of the cunning devil that jerked his strings?
Is that one idle, now that the strings are cut?

The man's body will rot under lime, and that soon.
But the parades have taught his uniform to march.
The hunters close in: do they feel the danger?
When they wrench his body to pieces, will they hear
A sigh as his spirit is sucked into the air
That they must breathe? And will his uniform
March on, march on, across Europe? Will their children
Hop in the streets like cool sparrows, and draw
His spirit into their hopeful lungs? Will
Their hearts jingle with hate? And who shall save them
If after all the years and all the deaths
They find a world still pitiless, a street
Where no grass of love grows over the hard stones?

John Wain

Timothy Winters

Timothy Winters comes to school
With eyes as wide as a football-pool,
Ears like bombs and teeth like splinters:
A blitz of a boy is Timothy Winters.

His belly is white, his neck is dark,
And his hair is an exclamation-mark.
His clothes are enough to scare a crow
And through his britches the blue winds blow.

When teacher talks he won't hear a word
And he shoots down dead the arithmetic-bird,
He licks the patterns off his plate
And he's not even heard of the Welfare State.

Timothy Winters has bloody feet
And he lives in a house on Suez Street,
He sleeps in a sack on the kitchen floor
And they say there aren't boys like him any more.

Old Man Winters likes his beer
And his missus ran off with a bombardier
Grandma sits in the grate with a gin
And Timothy's dosed with an aspirin.

The Welfare Worker lies awake
But the law's as tricky as a ten-foot snake,
So Timothy Winters drinks his cup
And slowly goes on growing up.

At Morning Prayers the Headmaster helves[1]
For children less fortunate than ourselves,
And the loudest response in the room is when
Timothy Winters roars 'Amen!'

So come one angel, come on ten:
Timothy Winters says 'Amen
Amen amen amen amen.'
Timothy Winters, Lord.

     Amen.

       Charles Causley

---

[1] helves: talks at length and more than necessary.

'Oh lost and lonely one'   6

Press Association Ltd: Harold Thompson of Brierley Hill, Staffs

To a small boy who died at Diepkloof Reformatory

Small offender, small innocent child
With no conception or comprehension
Of the vast machinery set in motion
By your trivial transgression,
Of the great forces of authority,
Of judges, magistrates and lawyers,
Psychologists, psychiatrists, and doctors,
Principals, police, and sociologists,
Kept moving and alive by your delinquency,
This day, and under the shining sun
Do I commit your body to the earth
Oh child, oh lost and lonely one.

Clerks are moved to action by your dying;
Your documents, all neatly put together,
Are transferred from the living to the dead,
Here is the document of birth
Saying that you were born and where and when,
But giving no hint of joy or sorrow,
Or if the sun shone, or if the rain was falling,
Or what bird flew singing over the roof
Where your mother travailed. And here your name
Meaning in white man's tongue, he is arrived,
But to what end or purpose is not said.

Here is the last certificate of Death;
Forestalling authority he sets you free,
You that did once arrive are now departed
And are enfolded in the sole embrace
Of kindness that earth ever gave to you.
So negligent in life, in death belatedly
She pours her generous abundance on you
And rains her bounty on the quivering wood
And swaddles you about, where neither hail nor tempest,
Neither wind nor snow nor any heat of sun
Shall now offend you, and the thin cold spears

Of the highveld[1] rain that once so pierced you
In falling on your grave shall press you closer
To the deep repentant heart.

Here is the warrant of committal,
For this offence, oh small and lonely one,
For this offence in whose commission
Millions of men are in complicity
You are committed. So do I commit you,
Your frail body to the waiting ground,
Your dust to the dust of the veld,—
Fly home-bound soul to the great Judge-President
Who, unencumbered by the pressing need
To give society protection, may pass on you
The sentence of the indeterminate compassion.

Alan Paton

African beggar

Sprawled in the dust outside the Syrian store,
a target for small children, dogs and flies,
a heap of verminous rags and matted hair,
he watches us with cunning, reptile eyes,
his noseless, smallpoxed face creased in a sneer.

Sometimes he shows his yellow stumps of teeth
and whines for alms, perceiving that we bear
the curse of pity; a grotesque mask of death,
with hands like claws about his begging-bowl.

But often he is lying all alone
within the shadow of a crumbling wall,
lost in the trackless jungle of his pain,
clutching the pitiless red earth in vain
and whimpering like a stricken animal.

Raymond Tong

[1] highveld: open, mostly treeless, grassland in South Africa.

The hunchback in the park

The hunchback in the park
A solitary mister
Propped between trees and water
From the opening of the garden lock
That lets the trees and water enter
Until the Sunday sombre bell at dark

Eating bread from a newspaper
Drinking water from the chained cup
That the children filled with gravel
In the fountain basin where I sailed my ship
Slept at night in a dog kennel
But nobody chained him up.

Like the park birds he came early
Like the water he sat down
And Mister they called hey Mister
The truant boys from the town
Running when he had heard them clearly
On out of sound

Past lake and rockery
Laughing when he shook his paper
Hunchbacked in mockery
Through the loud zoo of the willow groves
Dodging the park keeper
With his stick that picked up leaves.

And the old dog sleeper
Alone between nurses and swans
While the boys among willows
Made the tigers jump out of their eyes
To roar on the rockery stones
And the groves were blue with sailors

Made all day until bell time
A woman figure without fault
Straight as a young elm
Straight and tall from his crooked bones
That she might stand in the night
After the locks and chains

All night in the unmade park
After the railings and shrubberies
The birds the grass the trees the lake
And the wild boys innocent as strawberries
Had followed the hunchback
To his kennel in the dark.

Dylan Thomas

Lousy Peter

1   Lousy Peter

Lousy Peter's terror was the Workhouse;
   In the summer, he preferred to sleep on a flat cold pavement
   With his back against a railing.
   When the sun rose, he stood up,
Strode into the gold glory like a lion,
Shook the slumber from his limbs,
Shook his mane and rough patched clothing worn in layers;
   Begging crusts of bread that had been meant for the birds,
   And scraps of meat,
   Until at noon he munched with his beard,
     Lying in a patch of sunlight,
The mob of town-boys came to pester him, to pelt him,
   Whirling round him as planets round a sun,
   Jostling him, jumping up and down,
   Their strident young voices tearing the air, mocking him,
As they shout 'Lazy Peter!' 'Crazy Peter!' 'Lousy Peter!'
     'Lousy Peter!'

2   *In the cold winter*

In the cold winter,
   At the edge where the town turned to country
   And his brother the scarecrow guarded the fields from rooks,
   And the lamps stopped blossoming altogether,
   He slept under straw in a barn
   Where the owl screeched and the mice nibbled the grain.
He would sleep late, then, stirring under the straw,
He, a sleepy warm bear, would sway
Clumsily on to his feet, would beg his way
By the cold festoons of ivy, knocking at doors,
   Whining, asked for bread,
   Until it was time to return at night,
   Home to the straw
   Under a frosty moon.

3   *Frosty question*

If Lousy Peter's chief terror was the Workhouse,
   Next
      Came charitable ladies:
Professional beggar, he preferred to beg
    From unprofessional givers.
He knew the frosty questions—but not the answers,
The snow-cold reasonableness, burning like snow,
The compelling kindness. He better liked
A house where a barking dog denounced an enemy,
And a voice called into the night,
   'Damn you, who are you?
               Who are you?'
But, again, he did not know the answer.

Osbert Sitwell

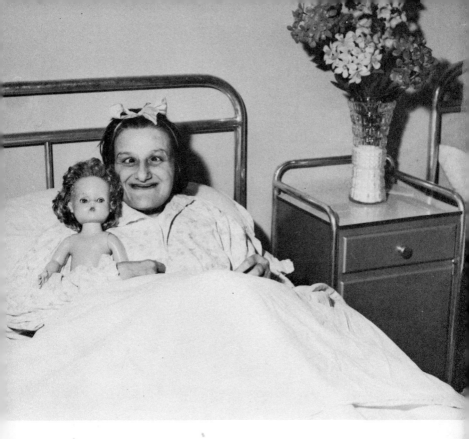

'*A matter hard to understand*'

7

Fur and feather

He can't touch feathers. He can touch fur.
An old man now, but all his life
He's been that way. He fell in love.
The young woman made no demur,
And married him. He and his wife
Raised a family, since gone
To the world's ends. Then he lost her,
And now he mostly lives alone
Writing to where his children rove
When he gets an address. But still
He cleans his pipe with a woollen thread
And dare not use a chicken-quill
To oil the grandfather clock. Absurd,
This lifelong something, this blood-taboo
That will not let him handle a bird.
But watch him go out to the garden loo
You'll see the robins follow him there.
Further afield, by moor and hill
Where he likes to wander, no lapwing will bother
To droop a wing, to make him leave
His chosen path and take another.
But should he stoop to stroke a cat
It will spark with hate and disappear.
Dogs dislike the shape of his hat,
Or the way he walks. He tries in vain
To coax a squirrel or a mouse to hand,
And cows move off as he draws near.
It's a matter hard to understand.
No philosopher knows whether
He, or beasts, or birds in their fear
Are wrong, or why he can't withstand
Desire for fur, while dreading feather.

Richard Church

Warning to parents

Save them from terror; do not let them see
The ghost behind the stairs, the hidden crime.
They will, no doubt, grow out of this in time
And be impervious as you and me.

Be sure there is a night-light close at hand;
The plot of that old film may well come back,
The ceiling, with its long, uneven crack,
May hint at things no child can understand.

You do all this and are surprised one day
When you discover how the child can gloat
On Belsen[1] and on tortures—things remote
To him. You find it hard to watch him play

With thoughts like these, and find it harder still
To think back to the time when you also
Caught from the cruel past a childish glow
And felt along your veins the wish to kill.

Fears are more personal than we had guessed—
We only need ourselves; time does the rest.

Elizabeth Jennings

Hospital for defectives

By your unnumbered charities
A miracle disclose,
Lord of the Images, whose love,
The eyelid and the rose,
Takes for a language, and today
Tell to me what is said
By these men in a turnip field
And their unleavened bread.

[1] Belsen: an infamous and particularly brutal concentration camp in
Nazi Germany during the Second World War.

For all things seem to figure out
The stirrings of your heart,
And two men pick the turnips up
And two men pull the cart;
And yet between the four of them
No word is ever said
Because the yeast was not put in
Which makes the human bread.
But three men stare on vacancy
And one man strokes his knees;
What is the meaning to be found
In such dark vowels as these?

Lord of the Images, whose love,
The eyelid and the rose,
Takes for a metaphor, today
Beneath the warder's blows,
The unleavened man did not cry out
Or turn his face away;
Through such men in a turnip field
What is it that you say?

Thomas Blackburn

Mental sickness

Then this is being mad; there is no more
Imagining, Ophelias[1] of the mind.
This girl who shouts and slobbers on the floor,
Sending us frightened to the corner, is
To all the world we know now deaf and blind
And we are merely loathsome enemies.

It is the lack of reason makes us fear,
The feeling that ourselves might be like this.
We are afraid to help her or draw near
As if she were infectious and could give
Some taint, some touch of her own fantasies,
Destroying all the things for which we live.

[1] Ophelia: a young woman in Shakespeare's *Hamlet*, who goes mad.

And, worse than this, we hate the madness too
And hate the mad one. Measured off a space
There is a world where things run calm and true—
But not for us. We have to be with her
Because our minds are also out of place
And we have carried more than we can bear.

Elizabeth Jennings

Felo da sé[1]

'Thirty,' the doctor said, 'three grains, each one,
That's quite a lot of sodium-amytol!
Five, ten more minutes, and the job was done,
Just why do you think she wished to end it all?
Ah, well, that's not my business. You've her things?
Damn lucky that I had the stomach pump—
Take them up to her if the Sister rings.'
I thanked him and agreed the night was damp,
Then flicked through Punch and waited the event;
It was, you see, no time for sentiment.

Her things, though, had been much in evidence
Back in the flatlet when I searched through drawers
To find a nightgown (blue is for romance)
And her remembered hairbrush through such tears
As in these situations must be shed—
(It is the cause, my soul, it is the cause)
I found her slippers underneath the bed
Where we had . . . where she drained her bitter cup
In solitude the night before this night;
What mattered was to pack a suitcase up,
Put out the light, 'and then put out the light.'

[1] Felo da sé: literally means 'murder of himself', suicide.

64

'So,' the nurse said, 'you've come. She may go out.'
I noticed that my shoe-lace was untied,
But though some words climbed up into my throat
Found none appropriate to suicide;
I took her arm, though, like a helpful friend
And led her downstairs to the waiting car,
Thinking, our game we do not understand
Nor who is playing it or what we are,
Her landlord came in time and that was luck.
I changed the gear. Who drives behind my back?

Her friend was waiting for us at the flat
With tea and so on. This I had arranged.
Knowing too well such passion spun the plot,
Death was its end unless the scene was changed,
What could I do but tear apart the script
Which made quite clear the end of our impasse?
As, kneading with her hands, she sat white lipped,
(There are some shadows which take long to pass)
Her friend poured tea, and slowly, drop by drop,
In solitude we drained our acid cup.

We had exhausted words as well as touch,
Therefore at half past ten I said goodbye,
Breaking the silence with a lifted latch,
To join, once more, my own identity.
That night the chilly street was not as dark
With its faint lamp as my intelligence,
And since more suited is a question mark
Than a full-stop, to human ignorance,
The blue stone I recall on her left hand;
Just what it means I do not understand.

Thomas Blackburn

65

'When she had to sit beside a Negro'

8

Hypocrite

She spoke of heaven
And an angelic host;
She spoke of God
And the Holy Ghost;
She spoke of Christ's teachings
Of man's brotherhood;
Yet when she had to sit beside a Negro once—
She stood.

Elizabeth Hart

Telephone conversation

The price seemed reasonable, location
Indifferent. The landlady swore she lived
Off premises. Nothing remained
But self-confession. 'Madam,' I warned,
'I hate a wasted journey—I am African.'
Silence. Silenced transmission of
Pressurized good-breeding. Voice, when it came,
Lipstick coated, long gold-rolled
Cigarette-holder pipped. Caught I was, foully.
'HOW DARK?' . . . I had not misheard. . . . 'ARE YOU LIGHT
OR VERY DARK?' Button B. Button A. Stench
Of rancid breath of public hide-and-speak.
Red booth. Red pillar-box. Red double-tiered
Omnibus squelching tar. It *was* real! Shamed
By ill-mannered silence, surrender
Pushed dumbfounded to beg simplification.
Considerate she was, varying the emphasis—
'ARE YOU DARK? OR VERY LIGHT?' Revelation came.
'You mean—like plain or milk chocolate?'
Her assent was clinical, crushing in its light
Impersonality. Rapidly, wave-length adjusted,
I chose. 'West African sepia'—and as afterthought,
'Down in my passport.' Silence for spectroscopic[1]

[1] spectroscopic: related to the kinds of colours in the spectrum. Here
she is letting her imagination range over all the colours that exist.

Flight of fancy, till truthfulness clanged her accent
Hard on the mouthpiece. 'WHAT'S THAT?' conceding
'DON'T KNOW WHAT THAT IS.' 'Like brunette.'
'THAT'S DARK, ISN'T IT?' 'Not altogether.
Facially, I am brunette, but madam, you should see
The rest of me. Palm of my hand, soles of my feet
Are a peroxide blonde. Friction, caused—
Foolishly madam—by sitting down, has turned
My bottom raven black—One moment madam!'—
        sensing
Her receiver rearing on the thunderclap
About my ears—'Madam,' I pleaded 'wouldn't you rather
See for yourself?'

                                    Wole Soyinka

African question mark

Don't know why,
Black,
Must still stand with my back
To the last frontier of fear
In my own land.

Don't know why I now
Must turn into a
Mau Mau[1]
And lift my hand
Against my fellow man
To live in my own land.

But it is so—
And being so,
All I know:
For you and me
There's woe.

                                    Langston Hughes

[1] Mau Mau: terrorist political-group in Kenya. Aiming to expel all
white people from Kenya, they assassinated some white settlers.

Holding the line
Rhodesia 1962

Yes, ugly down there. Yes, when Roddy drove
The back way past the club the gangs were out
Breaking things up. He heard the windows go.
No, heard not saw. Now tell me—would you wait?
Why hang around? And after all, we knew
The thing was coming. Yes, it's pretty grave.

Mary, you know, was nearly raped. Two men
Became most threatening. No, I only heard.
She told old Bob. I got it all from Jack.
Jack's one of us. Yes, you can take his word—
He wouldn't make it up, he's far too thick.
My wife's afraid to sleep. I've got my gun.

Yes, quiet up here. Odd. But then I guess
They know they're in for trouble if they try.
What've I seen myself? Oh, nothing much.
Why stick one's neck out? All I want to say
Is this, old chap—that now we've got to teach
The bastards not to bounce. You're with me? Yes?

Edward Lucie-Smith

Bus boycott

Two hours walk to work and back.
Rolling their eyes and rolling slightly,
Loose as runners on running tracks,
At dawn setting off, they return nightly
To where their shanty chimneys thrust
Blackened funnels from roofs of rust.
Over the saffron, smoke-smeared veld,
Braziers gleaming in mauve-pink hollows,
Alexandra township's dust
Settles, as trilbies tilted, collars
Sodden, they slow up on the journey back.

71

Eight miles there and eight miles back.
Such exercise is beneficial,
Medical evidence is official
—though two hours walk on Kaffir beer,
Belching as the fortunate steer
Unsteady routes through blackleg cars
Offering lifts and opening doors
Usually closed, needs a clear
Motive to sustain the miles
Wearing down the twisted smiles.
Shoes in hand to save the leather,
At least they're certain of the weather
On the journey there and journey back.

Two hours there and two hours back.
Buses idle in their hangars,
Illustrate their only right,
To withhold custom from the white.
A penny busfare raise has proved
The straw upon the camel's back.
At check-points, passes are demanded,
Holding them up along the track
Of this ballooning dream that severs
Economic links that bind
The victim to his servile grind.
To-day will never be countermanded,
There cannot be a journey back.

Two hours there, and two hours back.
The glinting corrugated iron
Beckons in its smoking bowl,
Smells of mealie, smells of fear,
Which pedestrian workers share
With tsotsis[1] on their evening prowl
For retribution—an apprehension lying
Like thunder in the sinking air.

[1] tsotsis: black teen-age delinquents in the big cities of South Africa.

72

Sweating sourly, each relying
On a corporative idea,
Follows his nose, and follows freely
His instinct there, his instinct back.

Alan Ross

Incident

Once riding in old Baltimore,
Heart-filled, head-filled with glee,
I saw a Baltimorean
Keep looking straight at me.

Now I was eight and very small,
And he was no whit bigger,
And so I smiled, but he poked out
His tongue, and called me 'Nigger'.

I saw the whole of Baltimore
From May until December;
Of all the things that happened there
That's all that I remember.

Countee Cullen

'*Registered, licensed homicide*'

9

Beat that light!

I think the horses must be laughing,
Kicking up their heels and chaffing,
Watching from their green abode
The things that drove them off the road,
Whinnying in soft derision
At breakdown, blowout and collision,
Neighing, as they roam the prairies,
Motorists' obituaries.

Read the epitaphs on Monday
Of drivers various and Sunday;
Beep the horn and howl the klaxon
For Hebrew, Latin, and Anglo-Saxon;
Howling klaxon, beeping horn,
The funeral dirge of Monday morn,
Usher out the unlucky drivers
Without convincing the survivors.
Here's a curve and here's a truck,
Take a chance, and trust to luck;
The next one's practically standing still—
We'll pass it at the top of the hill.
That's the trick, you're doing fine;
Now try cutting out of line!
What of the surgeon and mortician
If drivers drove without ambition?

Every one-horse-power mind has bought
Its ninety-horse-power juggernaut[1]
And rideth handsome, high and wide
In registered, licensed homicide,
Thus solving neatly throughout the nation
The problem of over-population.
What is that sound that follows after?
The echo, my friend, of equine laughter.

Ogden Nash

[1] juggernaut: Hindu idol carried on wheels in certain festivals. Faithful
Hindus were said to throw themselves under its wheels.

To the station

                           'Bye
                           dear,
                           no, I
                           won't
                           drive
                           fast.
Remember (I keep saying with a
look at the dashboard clock which
is probably a bit slow as usual)
          accidents can be
                    caused by people
                              like YOU, you dim
                                   blonde crawling Mum
                                        in the middle of the
                                        road with your kinder-
                                        garten-bound load of tod-
                              dlers. Trouble with (*and* you!)
                    most motorists they have no
          sense of destination, not to say any
feeling for others who are fighting
                                   time
                                   as
                                   they
                                   nip
                         between wobbly
               cyclists and slew-parked
          vans, and this sand and gravel
truck suddenly
          halting with
                    no warning of any
                              kind and opens
                                        his
                                        door
                                        and
                                        serve
                                        him
                                        right

                              if I'd damned-
well killed him. I suppose I can
risk fifty along this bit, no cops
in sight, two minutes to go and I
can make it if I put my foot down
                              and
                              pass
                              this
                              tree-
                              cutting machine
                              on its near
                                        side

            a close
         thing, that,
what the hell, I made it. Got
to take a chance now and then
or miss the confounded train, look
out you FOOL in that convertible . .
                         Hello
                         nurse
                         where am I?
                                   J. B. Boothroyd

Meditation on the A30

A man on his own in a car
    Is revenging himself on his wife;
He opens the throttle and bubbles with dottle
    And puffs at his pitiful life.

'She's losing her looks very fast,
    She loses her temper all day;
That lorry won't let me get past,
    This Mini is blocking my way.

'Why can't you step on it and shift her!
    I can't go on crawling like this!
At breakfast she said that she wished I was dead—
    Thank heavens we don't have to kiss.

'I'd like a nice blonde on my knee
   And one who won't argue or nag.
Who dares to come hooting at *me*?
   I only give way to a Jag.

'You're barmy or plastered, I'll pass you, you bastard—
   I *will* overtake you. I *will!*'
As he clenches his pipe, his moment is ripe
   And the corner's accepting its kill.

John Betjeman

'No more to build on there'

10

'Out, out—'

The buzz saw snarled and rattled in the yard
And made dust and dropped stove-length sticks of wood,
Sweet-scented stuff when the breeze drew across it.
And from there those that lifted eyes could count
Five mountain ranges one behind the other
Under the sunset far into Vermont.
And the saw snarled and rattled, snarled and rattled,
As it ran light, or had to bear a load.
And nothing happened: day was all but done.
Call it a day, I wish they might have said
To please the boy by giving him the half hour
That a boy counts so much when saved from work.
His sister stood beside them in her apron
To tell them 'Supper'. At the word, the saw,
As if to prove saws knew what supper meant,
Leapt out at the boy's hand, or seemed to leap—
He must have given the hand. However it was,
Neither refused the meeting. But the hand!
The boy's first outcry was a rueful laugh,
As he swung toward them holding up the hand
Half in appeal, but half as if to keep
The life from spilling. Then the boy saw all—
Since he was old enough to know, big boy
Doing a man's work, though a child at heart—
He saw all spoiled. 'Don't let him cut my hand off—
The doctor, when he comes. Don't let him, sister!'
So. But the hand was gone already.
The doctor put him in the dark of ether.
He lay and puffed his lips out with his breath.
And then—the watcher at his pulse took fright.
No one believed. They listened at his heart.
Little—less—nothing!—and that ended it.
No more to build on there. And they, since they
Were not the one dead, turned to their affairs.

Robert Frost

Death on a live wire

Treading a field I saw afar
A laughing fellow climbing the cage
That held the grinning tensions of wire,
Alone, and no girl gave him courage.

Up he climbed on the diamond struts,
Diamond cut diamond, till he stood
With the insulators brooding like owls
And all their live wisdom, if he would.

I called to him climbing and asked him to say
What thrust him into the singeing sky:
The one word he told me the wind took away,
So I shouted again, but the wind passed me by

And the gust of his answer tore at his coat
And struck him stark on the lightning's bough;
Humanity screeched in his manacled throat
And he cracked with flame like a figure of straw.

Turning, burning, he dangled black,
A hot sun swallowing at his fork
And shaking embers out of his back,
Planting his shadow of fear in the chalk.

O then he danced an incredible dance
With soot in his sockets, hanging at heels;
Uprooted mandrakes[1] screamed in his loins,
His legs thrashed and lashed like electric eels;

[1] mandrakes: a plant with a root formerly supposed to resemble a human form. It was said to shriek when it was pulled from the ground.

84

For now he embraced the talent of iron,
The white-hot ore that comes from the hill,
The Word out of which the electrons run,
The snake in the rod and the miracle;

And as he embraced it the girders turned black,
Fused metal wept and great tears ran down,
Till his fingers like snails at last came unstuck
And he fell through the cage of the sun.

Michael Baldwin

The fifth sense

A 65-year-old Cypriot Greek shepherd, Nicolis Loizou,
was wounded by security forces early today. He was
challenged twice; when he failed to answer, troops
opened fire. A subsequent hospital examination showed
that the man was deaf. *News item, December 30th, 1957*

Lamps burn all the night
Here, where people must be watched and seen,
And I, a shepherd, Nicolis Loizou,
Wish for the dark, for I have been
Sure-footed in the dark, but now my sight
Stumbles among these beds, scattered white boulders,
As I lean towards my far slumbering house
With the night lying upon my shoulders.

My sight was always good,
Better than others. I could taste wine and bread
And name the field they spattered when the harvest
Broke. I could coil in the red
Scent of the fox out of a maze of wood
And grass. I could touch mist, I could touch breath.
But of my sharp senses I had only four.
The fifth one pinned me to my death.

The soldiers must have called
The word they needed: Halt. Not hearing it,
I was their failure, relaxed against the winter
Sky, the flag of their defeat.
With their five senses they could not have told
That I lacked one, and so they had to shoot.
They would fire at a rainbow if it had
A colour less than they were taught.

Christ said that when one sheep
Was lost, the rest meant nothing any more.
Here in this hospital, where others' breathing
Swings like a lantern in the polished floor
And squeezes those who cannot sleep,
I see how precious each thing is, how dear,
For I may never touch, smell, taste or see
Again, because I could not hear.

Patricia Beer

At 30,000 feet

A fleck of silver against the darkening blue
The hollow cylinder rockets under the sky's dome,
Unavailingly pursued by the thunder of its sound
Until that final scarlet reverberation;
Like the telegraphed words burning meaninglessly
Upon the slip of yellow paper, and the explosion
Of grief within the mind, this fire and thunder
Do not quite coincide:
The eyes of the watcher see the disaster
Before its voice awakens in his ear.

Nothing that has meaning descends again to earth;
The lighted runway waits vainly
To feel the screeching tyres;
Customs officials will not search this baggage
That downward flakes in dust on silent fields;
Hands cannot clasp, nor lips press
What is now blown weightlessly about the sky.

There was a moment when they drowsed
Deep in luxurious chairs;
Read magazines, wrote letters;
When stewardesses served coffee and liqueurs,
And dirty dishes were neatly stacked
In the bright kitchen.

No other moment followed;
Time stopped. There was nothing . . .

No doubt there is a meaning to this event;
But not the one that can be read
On the white face of the farmer
In mid-furrow gazing upward from his plough,
Nor in the burned minds of those who wait
At the airport barrier.

Bernard Gilhooly

The casualty

Farmers in the fields, housewives behind steamed windows,
Watch the burning aircraft across the blue sky float,
As if a firefly and a spider fought,
Far above the trees, between the washing hung out.
They wait with interest for the evening news.

But already, in a brambled ditch, suddenly-smashed
Stems twitch. In the stubble a pheasant
Is craning every way in astonishment.
The hare that hops up, quizzical, hesitant,
Flattens ears and tears madly away, and the wren warns.

Some, who saw fall, smoke beckons. They jostle above,
They peer down a sunbeam as if they expected there
A snake in the gloom of the brambles or a rare flower,—
See the grave of dead leaves heave suddenly, hear
It was a man fell out of the air alive,

Hear now his groans and senses groping. They rip
The slum of weeds, leaves, barbed coils; they raise
A body that as the breeze touches it glows,
Branding their hands on his bones. Now that he has
No spine, against heaped sheaves they prop him up,

Arrange his limbs in order, open his eye,
Then stand, helpless as ghosts. In a scene
Melting in the August noon, the burned man
Bulks closer greater flesh and blood than their own,
As suddenly the heart's beat shakes his body and the eye

Widens childishly. Sympathies
Fasten to the blood like flies. Here's no heart's more
Open or large than a fist clenched, and in there
Holding close complacency its most dear
Unscratchable diamond. The tears of their eyes

Too tender to let break, start to the edge
Of such horror close as mourners can,
Greedy to share all that is undergone,
Grimace, gasp, gesture of death. Till they look down
On the handkerchief at which his eye stares up.

Ted Hughes

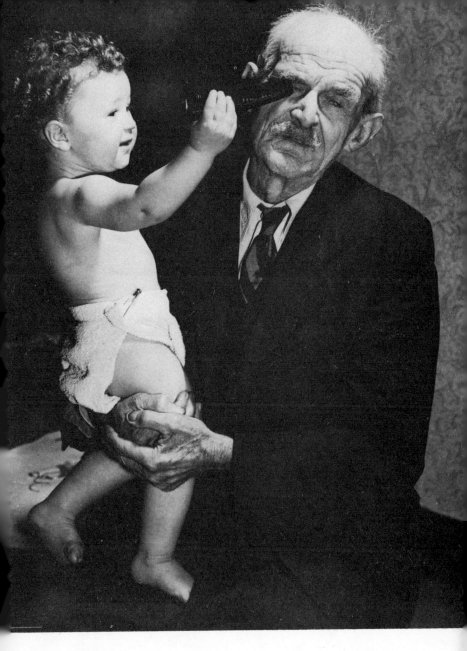

'The blight man was born for'   II

Keystone Press Agency Ltd: Father of 81 with son of 18 months

Spring and fall
to a young child

Márgaret, are you gríeving
Over Goldengrove unleaving?
Leáves, líke the things of man, you
With your fresh thoughts care for, can you?
Áh! ás the heart grows older
It will come to such sights colder
By and by, nor spare a sigh
Though worlds of wanwood[1] leafmeal[2] lie;
And yet you wíll weep and know why.
Now no matter, child, the name:
Sórrow's spríngs áre the same.
Nor mouth had, no nor mind, expressed
What heart heard of, ghost guessed:
It is the blight man was born for,
It is Márgaret you mourn for.

G. M. Hopkins

Blue girls

Twirling your blue skirts, travelling the sward
Under the towers of your seminary,[3]
Go listen to your teachers old and contrary
Without believing a word.

Tie the white fillets[4] then about your lustrous hair
And think no more of what will come to pass
Than bluebirds that go walking on the grass
And chattering on the air.

Practise your beauty, blue girls, before it fail;
And I will cry with my loud lips and publish
Beauty which all our power shall never establish,
It is so frail.

[1] wanwood: masses of leaves, yellow and pale.
[2] leafmeal: settling leaf by leaf (compare with piecemeal).
[3] seminary: a college.
[4] fillets: hairbands.

For I could tell you a story which is true;
I know a lady with a terrible tongue,
Blear eyes fallen from blue,
All her perfections tarnished—and yet it is not long
Since she was lovelier than any of you.

John Crowe Ransom

At Middle-field Gate in February

The bars are thick with drops that show
    As they gather themselves from the fog
Like silver buttons ranged in a row,
And as evenly spaced as if measured, although
    They fall at the feeblest jog.

They load the leafless hedge hard by,
    And the blades of last year's grass.
While the fallow ploughland turned up nigh
In raw rolls, clammy and clogging lie—
    Too clogging for feet to pass.

How dry it was òn a far-back day
    When straws hung the hedge and around,
When amid the sheaves in amorous play
In curtained bonnets and light array
    Bloomed a bevy now underground!

Thomas Hardy

Dick Straightup

Past eighty, but never in eighty years—
Eighty winters on the windy ridge
Of England—has he buttoned his shirt or his jacket.
He sits in the bar-room seat he has been
Polishing with his backside sixty-odd years
Where nobody else sits. White is his head,

92

But his cheek high, hale as when he emptied
Every Saturday the twelve-pint tankard at a tilt,
Swallowed the whole serving of thirty eggs,
And banged the big bass drum for Heptonstall—
With a hundred other great works, still talked of.
Age has stiffened him, but not dazed or bent,
The blue eye has come clear of time:
At a single pint, now, his memory sips slowly,
His belly strong as a tree bole.

He survives among hills, nourished by stone and height.
The dust of Achilles and Cuchulain[1]
Itches in the palms of scholars; thin clerks exercise
In their bed-sitters at midnight, and the meat salesman can
Loft fully four hundred pounds. But this one,
With no more application than sitting,
And drinking, and singing, fell in the sleet, late,
Dammed the pouring gutter; and slept there; and, throughout
A night searched by shouts and lamps, froze,
Grew to the road with welts of ice. He was chipped out at dawn
Warm as a pie and snoring.

The gossip of men younger by forty years—
Loud in his company since he no longer says much—
Empties, refills and empties their glasses.
Or their strenuous silence places the dominoes
(That are old as the house) into patterns
Gone with the game; the darts that glint to the dartboard
Pin no remarkable instant. The young men sitting
Taste their beer as by imitation,
Borrow their words as by impertinence
Because he sits there so full of legend and life
Quiet as a man alone.

He lives with sixty and seventy years ago,
And of everything he knows three quarters is in the grave,
Or tumbled down, or vanished. To be understood
His words must tug up the bottom-most stones of this village,

[1] Cuchulain: a hero of Irish legend, renowned for his deeds of valour.

93

This clutter of blackstone gulleys, peeping curtains,
And a graveyard bigger and deeper than the village
That sways in the tide of wind and rain some fifty
Miles off the Irish sea.

               The lamp above the pub-door
Wept yellow when he went out and the street
Of spinning darkness roared like a machine
As the wind applied itself. His upright walk,
His strong back, I commemorate now,
And his white blown head going out between a sky and an earth
That were bundled into placeless blackness, the one
Company of his mind.

Obit.

Now, you are strong as the earth you have entered.

This is a birthplace picture. Green into blue
The hills run deep and limpid. The weasel's
Berry-eyed red lock-head, gripping the dream
That holds good, goes lost in the heaved calm

Of the earth you have entered.

Ted Hughes

'Our vast collective madness'

12

Fox Photos Ltd: Playing roulette in Monte Carlo

Money-madness

Money is our madness, our vast collective madness.

And of course, if the multitude is mad
the individual carries his own grain of insanity around with him.

I doubt if any man living hands out a pound note without a pang;
and a real tremor, if he hands out a ten-pound note.

We quail, money makes us quail.
It has got us down, we grovel before it in strange terror.
And no wonder, for money has a fearful cruel power among men.

But it is not money we are so terrified of,
it is the collective money-madness of mankind.
For mankind says with one voice: How much is he worth?
Has he no money? Then let him eat dirt, and go cold.—

And if I have no money, they will give me a little bread so I do
     not die,
but they will make me eat dirt with it.
I shall have to eat dirt, I shall have to eat dirt if I have no money.

It is that that I am frightened of.
And that fear can become a delirium.
It is fear of my money-mad fellow-men.

We must have some money
to save us from eating dirt.

And this is all wrong.

Bread should be free,
shelter should be free,
fire should be free,
to all and anybody, all and anybody, all over the world.

97

We must regain our sanity about money
before we start killing one another about it.
It's one thing or the other.

D. H. Lawrence

Money

I am your master and your master's master,
I am the dragon's teeth which you have sown
In the field of dead men's and of live men's bones.

I am the moving belt you cannot turn from:
The threat behind the smiling of the clock:
The paper on which your days are signed and witnessed
Which only the mouse and the moth and the flame
    dare devour.

I am the rustle of bank-notes in your graves,
The crackle of lawyers' seals beneath your tombstones,
Borne to the leaning ears of legatees.

I am the cunning one whose final cunning
Was to buy grace, to corner loveliness,
To make a bid for beauty and to win it
And lock it away.

A. S. J. Tessimond

Wages

The wages of work is cash.
The wages of cash is want more cash.
The wages of want more cash is vicious competition.
The wages of vicious competition is—the world we live in.

The work-cash-want circle is the viciousest circle
that ever turned men into fiends.

Earning a wage is a prison occupation
and a wage-earner is a sort of gaol-bird.
Earning a salary is a prison overseer's job,
a gaoler instead of a gaol-bird.

Living on your income is strolling grandly outside the prison
in terror lest you have to go in. And since the work-prison covers
almost every scrap of the living earth, you stroll up and down
on a narrow beat, about the same as a prisoner taking his exercise.

This is called universal freedom.

D. H. Lawrence

Jigsaw II

Property! Property! Let us extend
Soul and body without end:
A box to live in, with airs and graces,
A box on wheels that shows its paces,
A box that talks or that makes faces,
And curtains and fences as good as the neighbours'
To keep out the neighbours and keep us immured
Enjoying the cold canned fruit of our labours
In a sterilized cell, unshared, insured.

Property! Property! When will it end?
When will the Poltergeist[1] ascend
Out of the sewer with chopper and squib
To burn the mink and the baby's bib
And cut the tattling wire to town
And smash all the plastics, clowning and clouting,
And stop all the boxes shouting and pouting
And wreck the house from the aerial down
And give these ingrown souls an outing?

Louis Macneice

[1] Poltergeist: a noisy spirit who throws things about and breaks
objects.

99

Going anywhere?

The limousine that Mr L. S. Dee,
Tortured with ulcers and insomnia,
Works like a slave to earn enough to run,
Is indispensably related to
His job of marketing accessories
For the equipment used in setting up
The plant essential to producers of
An automatic measuring device
Particularly favoured by those firms
That specialise in intricate machines
For companies that make a certain type
Of electronic instrument designed
To regulate a mechanism required
By factories that supply materials
Used in the shaping of precision tools
Connected with the processes involved
In manufacturing refrigerators:
Cold comfort for such perishable foods
As now enrich the breakfast Mr Grim
Savours without conviction, being sick
From an anxiety neurosis due
To his employment in the firm that made
The limousine that Mr L. S. Dee,
Tortured with ulcers and insomnia,
Works like a slave to earn enough to run . . .

Richard Kell

Living? Our supervisors will do that for us!

Dankwerts, scholarship boy from the slums,
One of many, studied three years for the Tripos,
Honours, English; grew a beard, imitated the gesture
And the insistent deliberate (but not dogmatic)
'There!' of his supervisor. For a time
The mimesis[1] was startling. Dankwerts knew

[1] mimesis: mimicking.

100

Uncannily what was good, what bad.
Life and earning a living, extra muros, for a time afterwards,
Left him hard up: people in their ambiguity
Nuisances. A bracing need for self-justification
(And spot cash) drove some of the nonsense out of him:
He found a foothold in films, the evening papers,
With his photograph, up to the ears in steaks, or ivy,
In 'art' magazines. Passing over the metropolis
He ejaculates like a satellite, evaporates, and falls,
Albeit on to a fat bank balance of amoral[1] earnings.

Whereas his supervisor can be seen any Friday
Walking up Trumpington Street with an odd movement of the
    feet,
Still looking like an old corm, lissom, and knowing
Uncannily what's good, what's bad,
And probably rather hard up out of the bargain.

David Holbrook

Attack on the ad-man

This trumpeter of nothingness, employed
To keep our reason dull and null and void,
This man of wind and froth and flux[2] will sell
The wares of any who reward him well.
Praising whatever he is paid to praise,
He hunts for ever-newer, smarter ways
To make the gilt seem gold; the shoddy,[3] silk;
To cheat us legally; to bluff and bilk[4]
By methods which no jury can prevent
Because the law's not broken, only bent.

[1] Amoral: non-moral.
[2] flux: the waste matter that flows away.
[3] shoddy: the pulled-out wool from old woven garments.
[4] bilk: to cheat.

This mind for hire, this mental prostitute
Can tell the half-lie hardest to refute;
Knows how to hide an inconvenient fact
And when to leave a doubtful claim unbacked;
Manipulates the truth but not too much,
And if his patter needs the Human Touch,
Skilfully artless, artfully naïve,
Wears his convenient heart upon his sleeve.

He uses words that once were strong and fine,
Primal as sin and moon and bread and wine,
True, honourable, honoured, clear and clean,
And leaves them shabby, worn, diminished, mean.
He takes ideas and trains them to engage
In the long little wars big combines wage.
He turns his logic loose, his feelings flimsy;
Turns eloquence to cant[1] and wit to whimsy;[2]
Trims language till it fits his client's pattern
And style's a glossy tart or limping slattern.
He studies our defences, finds the cracks
And, where the wall is weak or worn, attacks.
He finds the fear that's deep, the wound that's tender,
And, mastered, outmanoeuvred, we surrender.
We who have tried to choose accept his choice
And tired succumb to his untiring voice.
The dripping tap makes even granite soften.
We trust the brand-name we have heard so often
And join the queue of sheep that flock to buy;
We fools who know our folly, you and I.

A. S. J. Tessimond

[1] cant: clichés, or affected, hypocritical language used by a particular group of people.
[2] whimsy: language that is odd and fantastic.

'*Forests of unbudding stone*'

13

To some builders of cities

You have thrust Nature out, to make
A wilderness where nothing grows
But forests of unbudding stone
(The sparrow's lonely for his boughs);
You fling up citadels to stay
The soft invasion of the rose.

But though you put the Earth in thrall
And ransack all her fragrant dowers,
Her old accomplice, Heaven, will plot
To take with stars your roofs and towers;
And neither stone nor steel can foil
That ambuscade of midnight flowers.

Stanley Snaith

The war against the trees

The man who sold his lawn to Standard Oil
Joked with his neighbours come to watch the show
While the bulldozers, drunk with gasoline,
Tested the virtue of the soil
Under the branchy sky
By overthrowing first the privet-row.

Forsythia-forays and hydrangea-raids
Were but preliminaries to a war
Against the great-grandfathers of the town,
So freshly lopped and maimed.
They struck and struck again,
And with each elm a century went down.
All day the hireling engines charged the trees,
Subverting them by hacking underground
In grub-dominions, where dark summer's mole
Rampages through his halls,
Till a northern seizure shook
Those crowns, forcing the giants to their knees.

I saw the ghosts of children at their games
Racing beyond their childhood in the shade,
And while the green world turned its death-foxed page
And a red wagon wheeled,
I watched them disappear
Into the suburbs of their grievous age.

Ripped from the craters much too big for hearts
The club-roots bared their amputated coils,
Raw gorgons[1] matted blind, whose pocks and scars
Cried Moon! on a corner lot
One witness-moment, caught
In the rear-view mirrors of the passing cars.

Stanley Kunitz

Harvest hymn

We spray the fields and scatter
　　The poison on the ground
So that no wicked wild flowers
　　Upon our farm be found.
We like whatever helps us
　　To line our purse with pence;
The twenty-four-hour broiler-house
　　And neat electric fence.

All concrete sheds around us
　　And Jaguars in the yard,
The telly lounge and deep-freeze
　　Are ours from working hard.

We fire the fields for harvest,
　　The hedges swell the flame,
The oak trees and the cottages
　　From which our fathers came.

[1] gorgons: the three snake-haired women in Greek mythology. Their look turned any beholder to stone.

We give no compensation,
  The earth is ours today,
And if we lose on arable,
  Then bungalows will pay.

All concrete sheds . . . etc.

John Betjeman

Housing scheme

All summer through
The fields drank showers of larksong;
Offering in return
The hospitality of grasses,
And flowers kneedeep.

Over those wide acres
Trooped the plovers,
Mourning and lamenting as evening fell.
From the deep hedgerows
Where the foam of meadowsweet broke,
The rabbits and mice
Peeped out, and boldly sat in the sun.

But when the oaks were bronzing,
Steamrollers and brickcarts
Broke through the hedges.
The white-haired grasses, and the seedpods
Disappeared into the mud,
And the larks were silent, the plovers gone.

Then over the newlaid roads
And the open trenches of drains,
Rose a hoarding to face the highway,
'Build your house in the country.'

Richard Church

Beleaguered cities

Build your houses, build your houses, build your towns,
  Fell the woodland, to a gutter turn the brook,
Pave the meadows, pave the meadows, pave the downs,
  Plant your bricks and mortar where the grasses shook,
  The wind-swept grasses shook.
Build, build your Babels[1] black against the sky—
But mark yon small green blade, your stones between,
  The single spy
Of that uncounted host you have outcast;
For with their tiny pennons waving green
  They shall storm your streets at last.

Build your houses, build your houses, build your slums,
  Drive your drains where once the rabbits used to lurk,
Let there be no song there save the wind that hums
  Through the idle wires while dumb men tramp to work,
  Tramp to their idle work.
Silent the siege; none notes it; yet one day
Men from your walls shall watch the woods once more
  Close round their prey.
Build, build the ramparts of your giant-town;
Yet they shall crumble to the dust before
  The battering thistle-down.

F. L. Lucas

Song of the open road

I think that I shall never see
A billboard lovely as a tree.
Indeed, unless the billboards fall
I'll never see a tree at all.

Ogden Nash

[1] Babels: buildings in which there is confusion and great noise. (See *Genesis XI*.)

108

'*This above all is precious*'

14

This above all is precious and remarkable

This above all is precious and remarkable,
How we put ourselves in one another's care,
How in spite of everything we trust each other.

Fishermen at whatever point they are dipping and lifting
On the dark green swell they partly think of as home
Hear the gale warnings that fly to them like gulls.

The scientists study the weather for love of studying it,
And not specially for love of the fishermen,
And the wireless engineers do the transmission for love of
    wireless,

But how it adds up is that when the terrible white malice
Of the waves high as cliffs is let loose to seek a victim,
The fishermen are somewhere else and so not drowned.

And why should this chain of miracles be easier to believe
Than that my darling should come to me as naturally
As she trusts a restaurant not to poison her?

They are simply examples of well-known types of miracle,
The two of them,
That can happen at any time of the day or night.

John Wain

A correct compassion

*To Mr Philip Allison, after watching him perform a Mitral
Stenosis Valvulotomy[1] in the General Infirmary at Leeds*

Cleanly, sir, you went to the core of the matter.
Using the purest kind of wit, a balance of belief and art,
You with a curious nervous elegance laid bare
The root of life, and put your finger on its beating heart.

[1] Mitral Stenosis Valvulotomy: operation to cut valves in the heart
because they have narrowed and therefore obstructed the blood flow.

The glistening theatre swarms with eyes, and hands, and eyes.
On green-clothed tables, ranks of instruments transmit a sterile
    gleam.
The masks are on, and no unnecessary smile betrays
A certain tension, true concomitant of calm.

Here we communicate by looks, though words,
Too, are used, as in continuous historic present
You describe our observations and your deeds.
All gesture is reduced to its result, an instrument.

She who does not know she is a patient lies
Within a tent of green, and sleeps without a sound
Beneath the lamps, and the reflectors that devise
Illuminations probing the profoundest wound.

A calligraphic[1] master, improvising, you invent
The first incision, and no poet's hesitation
Before his snow-blank page mars your intent:
The flowing stroke is drawn like an uncalculated inspiration.

A garland of flowers unfurls across the painted flesh.
With quick precision the arterial forceps click.
Yellow threads are knotted with a simple flourish.
Transfused, the blood preserves its rose, though it is sick.

Meters record the blood, measure heart-beats, control the breath.
Hieratic[2] gesture: scalpel bares a creamy rib; with pincer knives
The bone quietly is clipped, and lifted out. Beneath,
The pink, black-mottled lung like a revolted creature heaves,

    [1] calligraphic: this adjective usually refers to beautiful handwriting.
Here it refers to the surgeon's dexterity in 'writing' his incisions on the
patient.
    [2] Hieratic: priestly.

Collapses; as if by extra fingers is neatly held aside
By two ordinary egg-beaters, kitchen tools that curve
Like extraordinary hands. Heart, laid bare, silently beats. It can hide
No longer yet is not revealed.—'A local anaesthetic in the cardiac[1]
    nerve.'

Now, in firm hands that quiver with a careful strength,
Your knife feels through the heart's transparent skin; at first,
Inside the pericardium,[2] slit down half its length,
The heart, black-veined, swells like a fruit about to burst,

But goes on beating, love's poignant image bleeding at the dart
Of a more grievous passion, as a bird, dreaming of flight, sleeps on
Within its leafy cage.—'It generally upsets the heart
A bit, though not unduly, when I make the first injection.'

Still, still the patient sleeps, and still the speaking heart is dumb.
The watchers breathe an air far sweeter, rarer than the room's.
The cold walls listen. Each in his own blood hears the drum
She hears, tented in green, unfathomable calms.

'I make a purse-string suture[3] here, with a reserve
Suture, which I must make first, and deeper,
As a safeguard, should the other burst. In the cardiac nerve
I inject again a local anaesthetic. Could we have fresh towels to
    cover

All these adventitious[4] ones. Now can you all see?
When I put my finger inside the valve, there may be a lot
Of blood, and it may come with quite a bang. But I let it flow,
In case there are any clots, to give the heart a good clean-out.

Now can you give me every bit of light you've got.'
We stand on the benches, peering over his shoulder.
The lamp's intensest rays are concentrated on an inmost heart.
Someone coughs. 'If you have to cough, you will do it outside this
    theatre.'—'Yes, sir.'

[1] cardiac: concerned with the heart.
[2] pericardium: a fleshy sac which surrounds the heart.
[3] suture: a surgical stitch to sew up a wound.
[4] adventitious: accidental; not produced on purpose.

'How's she breathing, Doug? Do you feel quite happy?'—'Yes, fairly

Happy.'—'Now. I am putting my finger in the opening of the valve.
I can only get the tip of my finger in.—It's gradually
Giving way.—I'm inside.—No clots.—I can feel the valve

Breathing freely now around my finger, and the heart working.
Not too much blood. It opened very nicely.
I should say that anatomically speaking
This is a perfect case.—Anatomically.

For of course, anatomy is not physiology.'
We find we breathe again, and hear the surgeon hum.
Outside, in the street, a car starts up. The heart regularly
Thunders.—'I do not stitch up the pericardium.

It is not necessary.'—For this is imagination's other place,
Where only necessary things are done, with the supreme and grave
Dexterity that ignores technique; with proper grace
Informing a correct compassion, that performs its love, and makes it live.

James Kirkup

Walking away
for Sean

It is eighteen years ago, almost to the day—
A sunny day with the leaves just turning,
The touch-lines new-ruled—since I watched you play
Your first game of football, then, like a satellite
Wrenched from its orbit, go drifting away

Behind a scatter of boys. I can see
You walking away from me towards the school
With the pathos of a half-fledged thing set free
Into a wilderness, the gait of one
Who finds no path where the path should be.

That hesitant figure, eddying away
Like a winged seed loosened from its parent stem,
Has something I never quite grasp to convey
About nature's give-and-take—the small, the scorching
Ordeals which fire one's irresolute clay.

I have had worse partings, but none that so
Gnaws at my mind still. Perhaps it is roughly
Saying what God alone could perfectly show—
How selfhood begins with a walking away,
And love is proved in the letting go.

C. Day Lewis

Masters

That horse whose rider fears to jump will fall,
Riflemen miss if orders sound unsure;
They only are secure who seem secure;
    Who lose their voice, lose all.

Those whom heredity or guns have made
Masters, must show it by a common speech;
Expected words in the same tone from each
    Will always be obeyed.

Likewise with stance, with gesture, and with face;
No more than mouth need move when words are said,
No more than hand to strike, or point ahead;
    Like slaves, limbs learn their place.

In triumph as in mutiny unmoved,
These make their public act their private good,
Their words in lounge or courtroom understood,
    But themselves never loved.

The eye that will not look, the twitching cheek,
The hands that sketch what mouth would fear to own,
Only these make us known, and we are known
    Only as we are weak:

By yielding mastery the will is freed,
For it is by surrender that we live,
And we are taken if we wish to give,
    Are needed if we need.

Kingsley Amis

Three wishes

I think of children with sad eyes
the dead the living the unborn
coins that pay for human choice
whose mothers mourn

I wish for your compassion enough
no cause for grief
and a talent with which to relieve
the dearth of love.

Karen Gershon

Index of first lines

A fleck of silver against the darkening blue   86
A man on his own in a car   79
All summer through   107
At the station exit, my bundle in hand,   12

Barely a twelvemonth after   21
Build your houses, build your houses, build your towns,   108
By your unnumbered charities   62
Bye, dear, no I won't drive fast.   78

Cleanly, sir, you went to the core of the matter.   111

Dankwerts, scholarship boy from the slums,   100
Does it matter?—losing your leg?   30
Dolls' faces are rosier but these were children   39
Don't know why,   70

Farmers in the fields, housewives behind steamed windows   87

He can't touch feathers. He can touch fur   61
His wild heart beats with painful sobs   27

I am the man who gives the word,   22
I am your master and your master's master   98
I do not know—would that I knew!   27
I think of children with sad eyes   116
I think the horses must be laughing,   77
I think they will remember this as the age of lamentations   7
I think that I shall never see   108
It is eighteen years ago, almost to the day   114
It sailed across the startled town   6
I've lived in the ghetto here more than a year,   41
I was walking in a government warehouse   18

Lamps burn all the night   85
Lousy Peter's terror was the Workhouse;   56

Margaret are you grieving   91
Money is our madness, our vast collective madness.   97
Mourn not for the man, speeding to lay waste   4
My parents kept me from children who were rough   46

Once, after a rotten day at school   45
Once riding in old Baltimore,   73
Over the hill the city lights leap up.   47

Past eighty, but never in eighty years   92
Peach, Plum, or Apricot!   17
Property! Property! Let us extend   99

Save them from terror; do not let them see   62
Say this city has ten million souls,   39
She spoke of heaven   69
Small offender, small innocent child   53
Sprawled in the dust outside the Syrian store   54
Suddenly he awoke and was running—raw   28

Telling lies to the young is wrong   3
That horse whose rider fears to jump will fall,   115
That one small boy with a face like pallid cheese   46
The bars are thick with drops that show   92
The bomb burst like a flower   11
The buzz saw snarled and rattled in the yard   83
The hunchback in the park   55
The limousine that Mr L. S. Dee   100
The man who sold his lawn to Standard Oil   105
The outcome? Conflicting rumours   32
The Polar DEW has just earned that   19
The price seemed reasonable, location   69
The snow is the blood of these poor Dead . . . they have no other   37
The wages of work is cash.   98
Then this is being mad; there is no more   63
There was a tower that went before a fall   3
'Thirty,' the doctor said, 'three grains, each one   64
This above all is precious and remarkable,   111
This excellent machine is neatly planned,   17
This trumpeter of nothingness, employed   101
Timothy Winters comes to school   49
Treading a field I saw afar   84
Twirling your blue skirts, travelling the sward   91
Two hours walk to work and back   71
Two householders (semi-detached) once found,   15
Two neighbours, who were rather dense,   14

We spray the fields and scatter   106
We'd found an old Boche dug-out, and he knew,   29
What is it we want really?   5
When in the aftermath   11
Where have all the flowers gone?   30
Will it be so again   33

Yes, ugly down there. Yes, when Roddy drove   71
You have black eyes,   38
You have thrust Nature out, to make   105

List of poems

1

Telling lies to the young is wrong   *Y. Yevtushenko*　　3
Babel   *Louis Macneice*　　3
Of mourners   *Dorothy Livesay*　　4
Conclusion from Autumn journal   *Louis Macneice*　　5
Red balloon   *Dannie Abse*　　6
Epitaph   *H. D. Carberry*　　7

2

Hiroshima   *Angela M. Clifton*　　11
Hiroshima   *Stanley Snaith*　　11
No more Hiroshimas   *James Kirkup*　　12
Parable   *William Soutar*　　14
The unexploded bomb   *C. Day Lewis*　　15
This excellent machine   *John Lehmann*　　17
Peach, Plum, or Apricot   *Bernard Kops*　　17
Fifteen million plastic bags   *Adrian Mitchell*　　18
Your attention please   *Peter Porter*　　19
The horses   *Edwin Muir*　　21
The responsibility   *Peter Appleton*　　22

3

The airman   *R. C. Trevelyan*　　27
The scene of war: the happy warrior   *Herbert Read*　　27
Bayonet charge   *Ted Hughes*　　28
The sentry   *Wilfred Owen*　　29
Does it matter?   *Siegfried Sassoon*　　30
Where have all the flowers gone?   *Pete Seeger*　　30
After a war   *Michael Hamburger*　　32
Will it be so again?   *C. Day Lewis*　　33

4

The war orphans   *Edith Sitwell*　　37
Algerian refugee camp—Aïn Khemouda   *Alan Ross*　　38
Bombing casualties in Spain   *Herbert Read*　　39
Refugee blues   *W. H. Auden*　　39
Homesick   *Anonymous*　　41

5

The place's fault   *Philip Hobsbaum*　　45
My parents kept me from children who were rough
　Stephen Spender　　46
Incendiary   *Vernon Scannell*　　46
On the death of a murderer   *John Wain*　　47
Timothy Winters   *Charles Causley*　　49

6

To a small boy who died at Diepkloof Reformatory   *Alan Paton*　　53

African beggar   *Raymond Tong*   54
The hunchback in the park   *Dylan Thomas*   55
Lousy Peter   *Osbert Sitwell*   56

7
Fur and feather   *Richard Church*   61
Warning to parents   *Elizabeth Jennings*   62
Hospital for defectives   *Thomas Blackburn*   62
Mental sickness   *Elizabeth Jennings*   63
Felo da sé   *Thomas Blackburn*   64

8
Hypocrite   *Elizabeth Hart*   69
Telephone conversation   *Wole Soyinka*   69
African question mark   *Langstan Hughes*   70
Holding the line   *Edward Lucie-Smith*   71
Bus boycott   *Alan Ross*   71
Incident   *Countee Cullen*   73

9
Beat that light!   *Ogden Nash*   77
To the station   *J. B. Boothroyd*   78
Meditation on the A30   *John Betjeman*   79

10
'Out, out—'   *Robert Frost*   83
Death on a live wire   *Michael Baldwin*   84
The fifth sense   *Patricia Beer*   85
At 30,000 feet   *Bernard Gilhooly*   86
The casualty   *Ted Hughes*   87

11
Spring and fall   *G. M. Hopkins*   91
Blue girls   *John Crowe Ransom*   91
At Middle-field Gate in February   *Thomas Hardy*   92
Dick Straightup   *Ted Hughes*   92

12
Money-madness   *D. H. Lawrence*   97
Money   *A. S. J. Tessimond*   98
Wages   *D. H. Lawrence*   98
Jigsaw II   *Louis Macneice*   99
Going anywhere?   *Richard Kell*   100
Living? Our supervisors will do that for us!   *David Holbrook*   100
Attack on the ad-man   *A. S. J. Tessimond*   101

13
To some builders of cities   *Stanley Snaith*   105
The war against the trees   *Stanley Kunitz*   105
Harvest hymn   *John Betjeman*   106

Housing scheme   *Richard Church*   107
Beleaguered cities   *F. L. Lucas*   108
Song of the open road   *Ogden Nash*   108

14
This above all is precious and remarkable   *John Wain*   111
A correct compassion   *James Kirkup*   111
Walking away   *C. Day Lewis*   114
Masters   *Kingsley Amis*   115
Three wishes   *Karen Gershon*   116

ACKNOWLEDGEMENTS

African Universities Press, 'Telephone Conversation' by Wole Soyinka from *Reflections*, edited by Frances Ademola; Thomas Blackburn, 'Hospital for Defectives'; Jonathan Cape, 'Fifteen Million Plastic Bags' from *Poems* by Adrian Mitchell, 'Will it be so again?' from *Collected Poems 1964* by C. Day Lewis, 'The Unexploded Bomb' and 'Walking Away' from *The Gate* by C. Day Lewis; H. D. Carberry, 'Epitaph' from *Treasury of Jamaican Verse*; Chatto & Windus, 'Going Anywhere?' from *Control Tower* by Richard Kell, 'The Sentry' from *Collected Poems of Wilfred Owen*; Christy & Moore, 'Red Balloon' from *Poems, Golders Green* by Dannie Abse; Curtis Brown, 'Masters' from *A Case of Samples* by Kingsley Amis, 'This Above All is Precious and Remarkable' by John Wain, from *The Guiness Book of Poetry 1958*; Dent and Curtis Brown, 'Beat that Light' from *Many Long Years Ago* and 'Song of the Open Road' from *Family Reunion* by Ogden Nash; Dent, 'The Hunchback in the Park' from *Collected Poems* by Dylan Thomas; André Deutsch, 'Warning to Parents' from *Recoveries* by Elizabeth Jennings; Essex Music and Fall River Music, 'Where have all the flowers gone?' by Pete Seeger; Eyre & Spottiswoode, 'Algerian Refugee Camp —Ain Khemouda' and 'Bus Boycott' from *African Negatives* by Alan Ross; Faber & Faber, 'Refugee Blues' from *Collected Shorter Poems 1927–57* by W. H. Auden, 'Bayonet Charge' and 'The Casualty' from *The Hawk in the Rain* and 'Dick Straightup' from *Lupercal* by Ted Hughes, '44 lines from Autumn Journal', 'Jigsaws 11' and 'Babel' from *The Collected Poems of Louis Macneice*, 'The Scene of War: the Happy Warrior' and 'Bombing Casualties in Spain', from *Collected Poems* by Herbert Read, 'The Horses' from *Collected Poems* by Edwin Muir, 'My parents kept me from children who were rough' from *Collected Poems* by Stephen Spender; Bernard Gilhooly and P.E.N., 'At 30,000 feet' from *New Poems 1965*; Gollancz, 'Three Wishes' from *Selected Poems* by Karen Gershon; Heinemann, 'Housing Scheme' from *Collected Poems* by Richard Church; Higham Associates, 'Timothy Winters' from *Union Street* by Charles Causley; 'This excellent machine' from *Collected Poems of John Lehmann*, 'The war orphans' by Edith Sitwell, 'Lousy Peter' from *Poems About People or England Reclaimed* by Sir Osbert Sitwell; David Holbrook, 'Living? Our supervisors will do that for us!'; Hogarth Press and Mrs Elna Lucas, 'Beleaguered Cities' from *Time and Memory* by F. L. Lucas; Hogarth Press, 'The Airman' from *Aftermath* by R. C. Trevelyan; Cyril Hughes and P.E.N., 'A Ballad of Capital Punishment' from *New Poems 1957*; Elizabeth Jennings, 'Mental Sickness'; James Kirkup, 'Earthquake' and 'A Correct Compassion'; Lom Management, 'Peach, Plum or Apricot' from *The Dream of Peter Mann* by Bernard Kops; Longmans, 'Death on a Live Wire' from *Death on a Live Wire* by Michael Baldwin, 'The Fifth Sense' from *Loss of the Magyar* by Patricia Beer; Edward Lucie-Smith, 'Holding the Line'; McGraw-Hill, 'Homesick' from *I Never Saw Another Butterfly* edited by M. Volavkova, 1964; Macmillan, the Trustees of the Hardy Estate and the Macmillan Company of Canada, 'At Middle-field Gate in

February' from *The Collected Poems of Thomas Hardy*; Macmillan, the Macmillan Company of Canada and Philip Hobsbaum, 'The Place's Fault' from *The Place's Fault and other poems*; Macmillan, the Macmillan Company of Canada and John Wain, 'On the Death of a Murderer' from *Weep Before God*; Methuen, 'The Responsibility' by Peter Appleton from *Talking About* by A. Percival and B. Bryan; John Murray, 'Harvest Hymn' and 'Meditation on the A30' from *Collected Poems* by John Betjeman; National Library of Scotland, 'Parable' by William Soutar; Northern House Pamphlet Poets, 'After a War' by Michael Hamburger; Harold Ober Associates, 'African Question Mark' from *Phylon* by Langston Hughes; Oxford University Press, 'Spring and Fall' from *Collected Poems* by Gerard Manley Hopkins; Alan Paton, 'To a small boy who died at Diepkloof Reformatory'; Penguin, 'Of Mourners' from *The Penguin Book of Canadian Verse* by Dorothy Livesay, 'Telling lies to the young is wrong' from *Selected Poems of Yevtushenko*; Laurence Pollinger and Holt, Rinehart & Winston, 'Out, Out' from *The Complete Poems of Robert Frost*; Laurence Pollinger and Little, Brown & Co., 'The War Against the Trees' from *Selected Poems 1928–58* by Stanley Kunitz; Laurence Pollinger and the Estate of the late Mrs Frieda Lawrence, 'Money-madness' and 'Wages' from *The Complete Poems of D. H. Lawrence*; Laurence Pollinger and Alfred A. Knopf, 'Blue Girls' from *Selected Poems* by John Crowe Ransom; Punch, 'To the Station', by J. B. Boothroyd, 'Fur and Feather' by Richard Church; Putnam, 'Felo da Sé' from *A Smell of Burning* by Thomas Blackburn; Routledge & Kegan Paul, 'Hiroshima' by Angela Clifton from *Poems by Children 1950–61*; George Sassoon, 'Does it matter?' from *Selected Poems 1908–56* by Siegfried Sassoon; Vernon Scannell, 'Incendiary'; Scholastic Magazines, 'Hypocrite' by Elizabeth Hart; Scorpion Press, 'Your Attention Please' from *Once Bitten, Twice Bitten* by Peter Porter; Stanley Snaith, 'Hiroshima' and 'To some builders of cities'; the Estate of A. S. J. Tessimond, 'Money' and 'Attack on the Ad-Man'; Raymond Tong and P.E.N., 'African Beggar' from *New Poems 1954*.

We should be glad to make the acknowledgement to Countee Cullen for 'Incident,' on receiving information.